FUZZY ST. JOHN

Our Fuzzy Q. Jones

by Bobby J. Copeland

Published by:
Empire Publishing, Inc.
3130 US Highway 220
Madison, NC 27025
Phone: 336-427-5850 • Fax: 336-427-7372
Website: www.empirepublishinginc.com

Other books by Bobby J. Copeland:

Best of the Badmen by Boyd Magers, Bob Nareau, and Bobby Copeland, published by Empire Publishing

Bill Elliott – The Peaceable Man, published by Empire Publishing

The Bob Baker Story, published by BoJo Enterprises

B-Western Boot Hill, published by Empire Publishing

Charlie King – We Called Him Blackie, published by Empire Publishing

Five Heroes, published by BoJo Enterprises

Gabby Hayes — King of the Cowboy Comics, by Bobby J. Copeland and Richard B. Smith, III, published by Empire Publishing

Johnny Mack Brown – Up Close and Personal, published by Empire Publishing

Roy Barcroft – King of the Badmen, published by Empire Publishing

Silent Hoofbeats, published by Empire Publishing

Smiley Burnette — We Called Him Frog by Bobby Copeland and Richard B. Smith, III, published by Empire Publishing

Sunset Carson —The Adventures of a Cowboy Hero, by Bobby Copeland and Richard B. Smith, III, published by Empire Publishing

Tim McCoy — A Real Rough Rider, by Bobby Copeland and Bill Russell, self-published

The Tom Tyler Story by Mike Chapman and Bobby Copeland, published by Culture House Books

Trail Talk, published by Empire Publishing

The Whip Wilson Story, published by BoJo Enterprises

Empire Publishing, Inc.
3130 US Highway 220
Madison, NC 27025-8306
Phone: 336-427-5850
Fax: 336-427-7372
Email: info@empirepublishinginc.com

Fuzzy St. John, Our Fuzzy Q. Jones © 2010 by Bobby J. Copeland

All rights reserved under International and Pan American copyright convention. No part of this book may be reproduced in any manner whatsoever without written permission from the publisher, except in the case of brief quotations embodied in reviews and articles.

Library of Congress Catalog Number 2010931073
ISBN Number 978-0-944019-57-3

Published and printed in the United States of America
1 2 3 4 5 6 7 8 9 10

TABLE OF CONTENTS

Dedication   4

What is a B-Western?   6

Love Those Sidekicks   7

Meet Fuzzy   8

Cowboying   16

Fuzzy with Fred Scott   19

Films with Don "Red" Barry   23

The Lone Rider Movies   25

Films with George Houston   27

Films with Bob Livingston   29

Billy the Kid Films   30

Buster and Fuzzy   32

Buster Crabbe Talks   34

Billy the Kid / Billy Carson Films   40

Lash and Fuzzy   42

Tidbits   48

Fans Remember Fuzzy   52

Fuzzy on Tour   61

Trail's End   67

Fuzzy's Obituary   69

Fuzzy in the Headlines   70

Essential Fuzzy   74

Fuzzy's Friends   79

Fuzzy in Action   80

Photo Gallery   113

About the Author   129

Selected Bibliographies   131

DEDICATION

to **John Brooker**

a B-Western fan from England
who spent many hours
viewing Fuzzy's movies.

His contributions to this book were invaluable.

With special appreciation to **Bill Russell** and **Richard B. Smith III.**

I would like to also dedicate this book to the many who have helped, influenced, and supported me in my endeavors and enjoyment of the Western film hobby:

        Boyd Magers
        Donna Magers
        Joe Copeland
        Bill Sasser
        Minard Coons
        Chuck Anderson
        Joe Konnyu
        Jim Hamby
        Buck Rainey
        Les Adams
        "Marshal" Andy Smalls
        Don Calhoun
        Dominick Marafioti
        Bill McDowell
        George Coan
        Don Key
        Rhonda Lemons
        Doneen Key
        Ron and Linda Downey
        Norman Kietzer
        Colin Momber
        Bruce Hickey
        Ralph Absher
        Burchell Thompson

And most of all, to my dear wife and faithful sidekick Joan, who doesn't mind me spending so much time "playing cowboy" – and, who sometimes plays cowboy with me.

WHAT IS A B-WESTERN?

If you were fortunate enough to have lived in the 1930s and 1940s – and if you were lucky enough to obtain a dime – you could visit your local movie house to view an exciting B-Western movie.

The B-Western is a true piece of Americana and reflects on a time when we believed in God, country, Mom, apple pie, and Saturday-matinee heroes. Many have asked, "Just what does the 'B' stand for in B-Westerns?" Well, it stands for budget – low budget. However, these films should not be thought of as inferior just because so little money was spent on making them.

To a great segment of the population, these little gems are still considered very special. They made an impression on the youths of that era that is still etched in the hearts and minds of those individuals today. In the 1970s and 1980s, fans of the B-Western gathered at Western film festivals to meet the performers, whom they had idolized as youngsters, in an attempt to recapture memories from the past. At these events, these fans enjoyed meeting in person Roy Rogers, Lash LaRue, Buster Crabbe, Rex Allen, Don "Red" Barry, Eddie Dean, Charles Starrett, Monte Hale, Sunset Carson, Clayton Moore, and many others.

The B-Westerns had simplistic and repetitive plots, and there was never a mystery about the identity of the hero or the villain. Everyone knew that there would be a rip-roaring movie climax, where good would triumph over evil, and that the hero would ride off into the sunset ready to fight another day.

The cowboy hero had the fastest horse, quickest draw, fanciest clothes, sang the sweetest song, and he possessed a heart of purest gold. Even on his worst day, he could beat the daylights out of the meanest bad guy and clean up the wicked town in the West -- without even getting dirty.

For decades, critics have maligned the B-Westerns and regarded them as nothing more than juvenile fare, or simply thought of them as a waste of film. Yet these grand old movies probably did more than any other one thing to shape ideas and ideals of that generation. The films provided action, comedy, music, and good wholesome entertainment for the entire family. They taught faith, hope, loyalty, honesty, and gave American's heroes. We knew the movies weren't real, but we loved them just the same. They made no attempt to show life as it is, but rather as life should be.

The B-Westerns were not a substitute for church, but they certainly complemented the message presented by the church. After watching one of these movies, you felt a tingle of goodness spread throughout your body . . . as if your soul had just been cleansed.

Unfortunately, the advent of television sounded the death knell for the B-Western films, and they are gone never to return. Gone now are Tom Mix, Buck Jones, "Wild Bill" Elliott, Allan "Rocky" Lane, Bob Steele, Hopalong Cassidy, the Durango Kid, and all the other heroes of the celluloid range.

Yes, our beloved B-Westerns are gone forever, but wouldn't it be fun if we could turn back the clock and start them all over again?

LOVE THOSE SIDEKICKS

What would the B-Western movies be without the sidekicks? The sidekicks were instantly recognizable and an integral part of Western film lore, not only for their entertainment value, but also because they offered an easy way for the director to make a point in a film. By listening to the hero discuss things with the sidekick, the audience got an insight into what the cowboy's intentions are without him having to continually talk to his horse or step out of character.

The sidekick's role was much different than that of the hero's. While the hero was usually erect, handsome and immaculately dressed, the sidekick was often stooped, homely, and sloppily attired. The sidekick was often superstitious, clumsy, famished, and physically and mentally challenged. The hero, by contrast, was near to perfection.
Many times, the sidekicks portrayed old prospectors or ranchers who have an intimate knowledge of the land for directions. And often, unwittingly, blurted out some save-the-day plan without even realizing it until the hero commends them on a great idea.

Usually, in spite of the hero's steadfast bravery or cleverness, the sidekick seemed amazed at his friend's abilities and courage. The sidekick might be lacking in bravery and brains, but his character was clearly good and true blue.

There were many sidekicks, but only a few really stand out. The most notable ones were George "Gabby" Hayes, Smiley Burnette, and Al "Fuzzy" St. John. Others along to provide a few laughs include Andy Clyde, Fuzzy Knight, Andy Devine, Max Terhune, and Dub Taylor. Although sidekicks, too, Raymond Hatton, Eddy Waller, and Richard Martin presented a more serious side.

The sidekicks played a valuable role in the old B Westerns, and we remember them fondly for their contributions.

MEET FUZZY

As "Fuzzy Q. Jones," Alfred St. John, the bewhiskered, loveable, scene-stealing little guy in the baggy pants, became one of filmdom's most popular sidekicks in spite of almost exclusive work in the cheap movies turned out by Producers Releasing Company and similar independents. Fuzzy found a place in the hearts of B-Western fans and never left there.

The big three of the cowboy comics has to be George "Gabby" Hayes, Smiley Burnette and St. John because they influenced the course of Western comedy – each in his own way. St. John was at it the longest; Burnette popularized the Western clown and made the sidekick nearly equal to the star, while Hayes refined the art of playing the foil, gave it humanity and a cantankerous dignity.

A Californian, born in Santa Ana on September 10, 1893, as Alfred St. John, our Fuzzy got his professional start at the age of 13 doing bicycle stunts at a local theater, later branching out into Vaudeville.

St. John entered silent films around 1913 and soon rose to co-starring and starring roles in short comedy films at a variety of studios. His uncle, Roscoe "Fatty" Arbuckle, probably helped him in his early days at Mack Sennett Studios. St. John was just the opposite of Arbuckle: he was slender, sandy-haired, nice looking, and a remarkable acrobat. It was reported he started in films for $3.00 a day.

(Note: Arbuckle was born Roscoe Conkling Arbuckle in Smith Center, Kansas on March 24, 1887.)

Many of the great silent clowns were also outstanding comic acrobats – and Al St. John was one of the best in the business. Being Arbuckle's nephew may have gotten him into the movies, but it was St. John's natural talent and agility that made him a star.

St. John usually played Arbuckle's fun-loving friend who often got Arbuckle into trouble by his mischievous behavior. During this period, St. John developed a "country rube" character to contrast to Arbuckle's screen role. His costume consisted of a

Roscoe "Fatty" Arbuckle, Buster Keaton, Al St. John, Alice Lake, THE COOK, Paramount (1918).

tight-fitting skull cap, a plaid shirt with a string tie, big floppy shoes, and checkered pants so big that they had to be held up by large suspenders. With two blackened teeth, this costume was a forerunner of his later Western sidekick appearances some thirty years later. He was once described as a "man with thyroid eyes whose ankles seemed to extend to his shoulders."

A trick bicycle rider and excellent all-around athlete, St. John was brought to Mack Sennett's Keystone Studios in 1914, where he played dozens of bit parts and occasional feature roles with Arbuckle – notably the Keystone Cops. When Arbuckle moved to Paramount in 1917, St. John followed. Together with screen newcomer Buster Keaton, the trio produced some of the funniest comedies of that era.

However, St. John's rise to stardom was derailed when Buster Keaton came aboard. One critic wrote that Keeton's falls were much better than St. John's. Obviously, competing with the remarkable Keaton was an impossible task.

(Note: The Keystone Cops was a series of silent film comedies about a totally incompetent group of policemen. The movies were produced by Mack Sennett for his Keystone Film Company between 1912 and 1917. The idea came from Hank Mann, who also played police chief Tehiezel in the first film before being replaced by Ford Sterling. The first Keystone Cops film was HOFFMEYER'S LEGACY (1912), but their popularity stemmed from the 1913 THE BANGVILLE POLICE, starring Mabel Normand.)

As early as 1914, Sennett shifted the Keystone Cops from starring roles to a background ensemble, in support of comedians like Chaplin and Arbuckle. The series served for supporting players Marie Dressler, Mabel Normand, and Chaplin in the first full-length Sennett comedy feature, TILLIE'S PUNCTURED ROMANCE (1914), as well as in MABEL'S NEW HERO (1913) with Normand and Arbuckle, MAKING A LIVING (1914) with Chaplin in his first screen appearance (pre-Tramp), IN THE CLUTCHES OF THE GANG (1914) with Normand, Arbuckle, and St. John, and WISHED MABLE (1915) with Arbuckle and Normand, among others.

Mack Sennett's Keystone film studio always used the spelling "Cops" whenever publicizing their films, never "Kops", as some more recent secondary sources have rendered the name. No contemporary citation of the "Kop" spelling has ever surfaced. Universal Pictures, however, changed the spelling to "Kops" in 1955 for the feature ABBOTT AND COSTELLO MEET THE KEYSTONE KOPS – which starred Sennett in a cameo role. In addition to those already mentioned, the Keystone Cops members have included Ford Sterling, Edgar Kennedy, Del Lord, Charles Avery, Bobby Dunn, Mack Riley, Slim Summerville, Chester Conklin, Malcolm St. Clair, A. Edward Sutherland, Edward F. Cline, Sydney Chaplin, Lige Conley, Henie Conklin, and Jimmy Finlayson.

In the 1916 picture, THE WAITER'S BALL, both St. John and Arbuckle are whacking away at each other with brooms when one broom breaks. The fight is halted while another broom is located, and then the scene resumed exactly as it left off. The two comics make a great scene out

Buster Keaton, Fatty Arbukle, and St. John.

of a broken shot. In another film, A DESERT HERO (1919) with Buster Keaton, St. John plays a hold-up man who suddenly breaks the gun Keaton is holding on him.

One might expect with all the twists and turns, tumbles and other gyrations performed in the movies that an accident could happen – and it did. On December 6, 1917, St. John was injured while filming, and had to be hospitalized. The injuries were not too serious because a couple of days later he was able to attend the funeral of a friend.

Sennett described one example of the rough-and-tumble incidents involving Hank Mann, (referred to by Sennett as his "toughest" comedian) and St. John. "Once when Hank was working with (Fatty) Arbuckle and Al St. John . . . he was supposed to be yanked out of the driver's seat of a wagon and land spread-eagled on the landscape. Then, Al was to jerk the pin from the singletree, and the horses were to pull Mann off the wagon. Al had trouble with the pin and was sweating and bawling. This delayed the action until the horses had picked up too much speed for such a stunt. When Al did get the pin out, the horses cut loose like runaway ghosts and snatched Hank 30 feet through the air, like a kite, until the law of gravity remembered him.

"By this time, Hank and the horses were almost out of Los Angeles County, certainly at least three whoops and a loud holler out of camera range. Hank descended into a plowed field, chin first, and furrowed a belly-whopping trench for 10 yards before, with considerable common sense, he let go the reins."

M. G. Cox, one of Sennett's performers, described an incident involving St. John: "Since Sennett didn't work from a script, whatever he thought was funny at the time was what we did. One day he asked us, 'Any of you ever been on roller skates?' We all just looked at one another. My friend Al St. John, who was the only one of the original Keystone Cops that had been a former stuntman, said he was pretty good on skates, but no one else knew how. It was my first time. So naturally Sennett sent over to a costume place and got twelve pair.

"We put them on and you should have seen the mess, Cops all over the place, falling, reeling, sprawling on the floor, running into each other. Billy Hauber said later he was on his feet only once in the whole scene. This was one time we didn't have to add any little business of our own to make the scene funny. It was genuine, every bit of it. And the Old Man, I guess Sennett must have about twenty-eight at the time, ran around egging us on, calling out instructions to his cameraman.

"When we were all exhausted and black and blue all over, he let us stop. I was really bruised up. We all were except Al St. John, but Sennett said it was one of the funniest pieces of film he'd ever seen."

St. John's first Western-flavored film came in 1918 when he played the role of "Wild Bill Hiccup" in a comedy satire of Westerns. Betty Compson was also in the cast, and it included that famous scene when Fatty Arbuckle performs his one-handed cigarette roll, striking the matches on a passing train and then leaping into the caboose as it passes by, stuff worth the price of admission, as one reviewer noted. St. John picked up on the cigarette rolling bit and incorporated it into his act for the rest of his life.

Fatty Arbuckle, Buster Keaton, and Fuzzy St. John (OUT WEST, 1918).

It was a big deal when, in July 1919, St. John signed a lucrative contract with Paramount. *The Los Angeles Times* carried the following report: "Knowing how to be funny on the screen depends on experience as well as an inherent humor and talent; so the raising to stardom of a comedian is a matter of interest. The latest funny man to be so elevated is Al St. John, long an associate of Fatty Arbuckle, who was yesterday announced by his manager, the ambitious Joe McClosky, to have bloomed as a first-magnitude luminary, under a contract just signed by him."

That same year, Fatty Arbuckle bought a minor-league baseball team, the Vernon Tigers. The team had been created in 1909 to compete in the six-year-old Pacific Coast League. On opening day, May 25, 1919, Fatty invited a large Hollywood contingent to watch in the sold-out grandstand. Tom Mix and his manager, Eddie Rosenbaum, occupied one box. *The New York Telegraph* reported: "Fatty, Al St. John, and Buster Keaton put on a side show. Dressed in the uniform of the home team, they staged a game all their own, a chalk bat and ball. The result when ball and bat met may be imagined."

Later St. John signed with Fox. When he did, he changed his screen image completely - from the country rube to a clean cut, wholesome, young sophisticated city slicker who wore white shoes with spats (a short cloth or leather gaiter worn over a shoe to cover the instep and ankle). In these movie shorts, he portrayed a level-headed character.

Although making a lot of money, things became unhappy at home causing St. John's wife to file for divorce. She stated her physician Elmer Anderson advised her to get the divorce in order to save her health. The divorce was granted in 1923. At that time, she was awarded alimony, an automobile, pay for a chauffeur, and $150 monthly for their daughter.

In 1924, St. John switched to Educational Studio where he made his Tuxedo and Mermaid comedy shorts. In STUDID, BUT BRAVE, St. John had to cross the country by a specified date in order to take advantage of a job offer, but he had no money. While crossing the country, he came across a gang of escaped convicts who stole his clothes and left their prison stripes behind. Rather than wear prison clothes, he wore his underwear and received many laughs as he went down the road with the sheriff on his trail. When a gang of runners came along, he joined the race, managed to win, grabbed the prize money, and took off again with the sheriff right behind him. The theater audience loved the movie.

After the 1923 divorce, he must have remarried and divorced again because in 1929 he was back in court, and the judge had him jailed for failing to keep up his alimony payments. St. John moaned: "I've been unemployed and faced with the obligation of keeping my mother and father, my first wife and adopted daughter (Mary Jane), and my second wife up. I'm doing the best I can."

Judge Burnell, who heard the case, was not sympathetic and sentenced him work on a road gang and ordered him to pay $1,642 in alimony arrears. St. John's friends and fans thought the sentencing unfair and started writing letters to the Judge on his behalf, even to the point of threatening the Judge's life. The letter writing campaign proved successful, and St. John was soon released.

(Note: St. John was not the only B-Western

sidekick to be sentenced to a road gang. In June 1942, Wally Vernon was also sentenced to a road gang for failing to keep up his alimony payments.)

In 1925 St. John stared in a movie, directed by Arbuckle, called THE IRON MULE. In the film, St; John throttles a small 1828-style steam locomotive through a rural period landscape, complete with inadequate trackwork, low tunnels, a makeshift barge and a raid by angry Indians. The locomotive is Keaton's model of Stephenson's engine "The Rocket" from OUT HOSPITALITY (1923), one of his feature films, and Keaton himself does a brief bit as an Indian. The humor in this comedy is more understated and subtle than the raucous rabble St. John usually inserts, and is a testament to his maturity as a comic actor, as well as to his long friendship with Keaton.

Later in 1920s, St. John was loaned out to other studios for small roles in feature films, but he became frustrated over the roles and returned to two-reel comedies. Later he was reunited with "Fatty" Arbuckle in some Vitaphone shorts that heralded Arbuckle's return to the screen, but St. John left the two-reel comedy shorts when Arbuckle died at age 46 in 1933. St. John's future would be in Westerns.

(Note: In 1921, Arbuckle threw a wild party – today we would call it an orgy – during Labor Day weekend. Bit player Virginia Rappe was injured at the party and died days later. Soon, Arbuckle was accused of raping, biting off one of her nipples, and accidentally killing Rappe. He endured three widely publicized manslaughter trials. His films were banned, his career was ruined, and he was publicly ostracized. Fatty was acquitted by a jury, and received a written apology, but the trial's scandal has mostly overshadowed his legacy as a pioneering comedian. Although the ban on his films was eventually lifted, Arbuckle only worked sparingly through the 1920s. In 1932, he began a successful comeback, which he briefly enjoyed before his death.)

Hillard Karr, St. John and Alice Davenport.

St. John made a lot of money while at Fox Studio, and had invested heavily in the stock market. When the market crashed in 1929, it is estimated he lost over $700,000.

(Buster Crabbe): "Fuzzy had made a lot of money, but when the stock market crashed he lost three quarters of a million dollars in a couple of days. He was buying stock on margin, which meant when the stock went down, you had to put in more money. Everything was all fouled up; they tried to get a hold of him by telephone but couldn't. They sold him out. All the money he thought he had he didn't have any more so he had to go back to work."

Al became so popular in the silent comedies and features that he was eventually making the incredible sum of $5,000 a week at Fox. However, with the advent of sound, Fox did not think an actor who specialized in pantomime and pratfalls would be successful in sound movies. The studio offered to buy St. John out at a fraction of his contract's worth. When he strongly objected and would not settle for less than what the full contract called for, he was eventually paid the entire amount. His refusal to take less money irked the studio, and they notified the other major movie companies that he was a troublemaker and that they should avoid hiring him.

While still associated with Fatty Arbuckle, they combined to make a hilarious short called BRIDGE WIVES (Educational Pictures, 1932). Arbuckle directed the film using the name William Goodrich. St John plays the featured role of the husband who goes crazy over contract bridge in the film. In reality, he was one of the film colony's most expert bridge players. He is one of the few players who has at various times held three perfect bridge hands, once having 13 hearts, once 13 clubs and at another time holding nine spades and three outside aces.

St. John's comedies were quite popular overseas. He is pictured here on the cover of a French magazine.

COWBOYING

Throughout the 1920s, St. John had been one of the most popular comedians working in films as evidenced by his large salary. However, the blacklisting by Fox was successful, and he was forced to accept minor roles for paltry salaries at the lesser-known studios. The switch to quickie Westerns and the huge reduction in salary must have been quite traumatic for the little comic.

His first real Western appearance was in May 1928 in the Tom Mix Fox silent film HELLO CHEYENNE. In the movie, he played a character named "Zip Coon." According to Larry Langman in his A Guide to Silent Westerns (Greenwood Press, 1992), this film could be the earliest example in which a known comic, in this case St. John, is used as the hero's sidekick strictly for comic relief. PAINTED POST, also released by Fox in 1928, was his second Western role, again with Tom Mix. When talkies came in, he returned to vaudeville for a short time but was soon back on the screen in an assortment of roles.

In addition to the Arbuckle comeback films, in 1930 he could be seen in Tiffany's LAND OF MISSING MEN, minus whiskers, as Bob Steele's semi-sidekick. At Tiffany, he supported Steele that same year in THE OKLAHOMA CYCLONE. In 1932, for the same studio, he again supported Steele, this time in RIDERS OF THE DESERT (World Wide). He made SONS OF THE PLAINS with Bob Custer at Syndicate in 1931, and worked in Monogram's LAW OF THE NORTH with Bill Cody in 1932. In 1933, he played an inept, fumbling, bumbling outlaw named "Bert" in John Wayne's Monogram release, RIDERS OF DESTINY. He and comedian Heine Conklin participated in a comedy routine in the film that, while amusing, broke the flow of the movie. In 1936, he was a stubble-beard sidekick to Tom Tyler in PINTO RUSTLERS at Reliable, and a bearded, tobacco-chewing sidekick to Rex Bell in WEST OF NEVADA at Colony.

In 1935-1936, St. John appeared in three Paramount *Hopalong Cassidy* films. He was in BAR 20 RIDES AGAIN (1935), billed as a character called "Cinco." In HOP-A-LONG CASSIDY (1935), he was billed 11th as a character called "Luke." And in TRAIL DUST (1936) he portrayed a character simply called "Al" and was billed 10th.

The Three Mesquiteers, created by William Colt MacDonald, was a popular series of books before it hit the movie screen. For reasons unknown, the first movie entry, THE LAW OF THE 45's (Normandy Pictures, 1935), only included two of MacDonald's characters, Guinn "Big Boy" Williams as "Tucson Smith" and St. John as "Stoney Martin." It is odd that St. John was billed as Stoney (with and "e") and Martin and instead of "Stony Brooke" which the character would be billed in future Mesquiteers films. The movie went virtually unnoticed, but has since become a footnote when writing about the Mesquiteer series.

(Note: Tim McCoy filmed seven non-Mesquiteers stories by MacDonald in 1932-1933.)

St. John continued to kick around at various studios and in undistinguished Western and non-Western roles until 1937 when he replaced Cliff Nazzaro as the comedy relief and became "Fuzzy" in the Fred Scott Spectrum series. He was in a number of films from 1937 to 1939, but primarily with Scott until he signed with Grand National to do a proposed series of trio films with Lee Powell and Art Jarrett. Only one film was made, TRIGGER PALS (1939), because Grand National ran into financial difficulties.

In 1937, St. John had joined Tex Ritter at Grand National for SING, COWBOY, SING. Just before Tex has a big brawl with Charlie King in the picture, King snarls the classic line, "This town ain't big enough for you and me." Later, when Tex is unjustly thrown in jail with St. John, Tex tries to clear his partner and slips in a private joke by saying to St. John, "Say, do you know what I tell folks down in my home town of Nederland, Texas when they get to feeling blue?" Tex then sings "Cowboy Medicine." The moviegoers probably had never heard of Nederland, Texas, but it really was Tex's hometown.

A great sadness hit Fuzzy in early July 1940 when his longtime friend and fellow actor and comedian Ben Turpin died of a heart attack. Fuzzy, along with an array of former silent-film comedians, attended Turpin's funeral. Turpin, the funny little man with the crossed eyes, always maintained that he could do a somersault from a standing start better than St. John or anyone else.

Fuzzy was really hopping in the early 1940s. In 1941 alone, he worked in three Bob Steeles, six George Houstons, two Buster Crabbes at PRC, and two Don Barrys at Republic. He also found time to work in two *Frontier Marshals* pictures. During the period of 1941 through 1946, he worked in a whopping 53 Westerns.

The PRC Westerns were unusual in several aspects. First, St. John played the same role in different series at the same time. This did not bother the fans at all. Second, the plots of the films were so simple that the screenwriters could crank them out at a rapid pace, and although the stories seemed alike, the comic work by Fuzzy prevented any complaint. The low-production qualities frequently provided some fine comedy by him that carried the films when the action and story did not. Despite great odds, Fuzzy made the films worth watching.

Author Bill Russell wrote, "If ever an actor had such a positive influence on a movie studio, certainly a producer of B-Westerns, it was Al St. "Fuzzy" John, master of pratfalls and one of the best sidekicks a star ever had. His screen portrayal of the character Fuzzy Q. Jones can safely be said to be the redeeming factor in the life of PRC pictures.

"Although PRC ranked low on the totem pole of production companies over a period of some 10 years, a number of cowboy heroes went through their gates. But it was Fuzzy who held them all together."

During 1941 and 1942, Fuzzy appeared in six Republic features starring Don "Red" Barry. He was not always Barry's sidekick in the films.

"It's old Blackie King, Fred. You can't trust him."

FUZZY WITH FRED SCOTT

(It was my pleasure to speak with Mr. Scott on the phone and to exchange letters with him. The last time I talked with him was when Harold Smith, promoter of the Knoxville Western Film Caravan, asked me to call Fred and invite him to the Festival. Scott thanked me but in a trembling voice said, "You do not know how much I would like to come but I've had some health problems, and my wife will not permit me to travel." I sensed he wanted to come so badly that he cried. He was pleased to do an interview and later wrote to me.)

Fred Scott talked about his career and Fuzzy: "Before I get to Fuzzy, let me say this – there would be no singing cowboys if it had not been for Gene Autry. He started it, and the rest of us were lucky enough to follow.

"I enjoyed my film career, but I enjoyed singing more. That is what I was trained for. I am often asked about my horse, if I did my stunts, other actors, and, of course, Fuzzy. I will start out talking, and please interrupt me if I get too far off the subject.

"Carl Mathews doubled for me in most of our pictures, and he was a great guy and a good actor. He often took his life and limbs in his hands in order for me to look good on the screen.

"Old White Dust (his horse) has been gone for many years. He was a fine companion. He wasn't one of the great trick horses, but he was a good actor and always knew his lines. (Laugh)

(Note: Scott's horse was sometimes billed as "White King".)

"I have to say a few words about Charlie King: He was in so many Westerns that we used to call them "Charlie King Westerns" – no matter who the star of the pictures was. Charlie was very versatile and always reliable. The minute you saw his face in a film and before he spoke the first word, you just knew he was up to no good. There was nothing subtle about Charlie.

"Some of my pictures were directed by Sam Newfield, and released under the banner of Stan Laurel Productions. Everyone knows of the great Laurel and Hardy comedy team. Stan was very much involved with the pictures. He financed them, and often came up with comedy routines for Fuzzy. At the time, Stan was involved with a French girl. He wanted her to play the lead in SONGS AND BULLETS (Spectrum). Well, she came on the set with a mink coat that Stan had just bought her. She was so proud of the coat that she wore it on set the first day of shooting. She knew nothing about acting, and stood with her back to the camera in that mink coat, and delivered her lines in broken English. She was attractive and not a bad actress. But she couldn't speak English. In the picture I say to Fuzzy, "Is that the kind of gal you would pick for a schoolmarm?" And Fuzzy says to me, 'Every time, boy!'

(Note: Fuzzy has another funny moment in the film when he Scott had the drop on some outlaws, he warned them: "All right, boys, I reckon you can take your hands down now, but don't try anything funny, or I'll jump down your throats with my spurs on and rake you from tonsil to toenail.")

"My pictures were done very cheaply. They are now referred to as B-Westerns, but mine should probably be called D-Westerns. The storylines were quite weak, and the films were shot very hastily. We would run through the scene before we shot it, but usually had only one chance to get it right. There was seldom a retake. One time, a cameraman forgot to load the camera before going on location. Well the whole company had to wait until he went back to the studio to get the film. This was time we had to make up. When you are scheduled to a complete a picture in approximately two weeks, making up time is not an easy thing to do. In the picture, Fuzzy and I harmonize, but he did not play the guitar – neither did I. It was played by someone else.

"Now more about that wonderful little man, Al St. John: I really feel like I am an expert on this great artist. It was my good fortune that he came into my life. Jed Buell, the producer of our first two pictures, had planned on Fuzzy Knight for my sidekick in MELODY OF THE PLAINS (Spectrum). However, Knight was tied up in a large picture at Paramount, so he was released from his commitment. Now nothing against Knight, but I was pleased to get Al for my sidekick. The name Fuzzy was already written in the script so they just kept it, and that's how Al got the name 'Fuzzy.' Later, I think it was his idea to add 'Q. Jones' to the Fuzzy name.

"I had seen Al in many of the Keystone Cops one-reelers from the silent days. I enjoyed his antics in those comedies – never thinking that someday I would meet him – much less work with him. Working with him was the easiest thing in the world. I never saw him lose his temper or heard him gripe about anything in all the time we were together.

"He was natural at the start – a great pantomimer, tumbler, and one of the greatest horsemen ever seen in Western pictures. He was one of the easiest people to work with that I ever met. He always had a twinkle in his eye, and could come up with something funny right on the spot. He knew his lines but was free to ad-lib, which he did brilliantly. Al was full of acrobatics, and could do amazing things without hurting himself. I don't recall him ever getting hurt by doing all the falls.

"I made other Westerns with other sidekicks, but missed old Fuzz. When C. C. Burr took over the production, he had his own people, and there was nothing I could do about it.

"I knew Al's first wife, and later I met his second wife (it was really Fuzzy's 2nd and 3rd wives). The first wife was a pretty good business person and managed Al's affairs. His stepson was an insurance agent one time.

(Note: Scott probably never realized just how astute Fuzzy's wife was at business. She handled the family's finances, and had a will prepared which left everything to her son by a previous mar-

riage. When she died, Fuzzy discovered that the will had left him practically broke.)

"By strange coincidence, Al lived across the street from us after I had retired from pictures, and I was in the real estate business. He used to scare the daylights out of Mary, my wife. Our house was one of the old Spanish types built around the turn of the century in Hollywood Hills near the hills where Valentino had his falcon lair. The living room had an 18-foot-ceiling, and the rooms were on different levels so that you stepped down, or up, to go to different levels of the house. Well, Al loved to put his hand out as if he were going to lean against a wall, but there was no wall there and his genius for acrobatics was such that we never knew if he was going to kill himself or not. It scared the life out of Mary and my daughters. But it was really funny! Later, after the family moved, I bought Al's old home.

"I liked Al tremendously as a person. So did everyone else. I don't know how much Al was paid, but I'm sure it was not enough. He was priceless. Al went on to work with another terrific athlete, Buster Crabbe, and they made a great team."

Fred Scott closed his interview by quoting a verse from one of his original songs, "The Golden Corral": "I hope when I die I will go to that land, when the last of the cold world I've trod, to be ridin' the range with that heavenly host in the eternal roundup of God."

(Note: Scott, like singing cowboys George Houston, Bob Baker, and Jack Randall, made no commercial recordings.)

The Fred Scott/St. John series was weak to say the least. The best was MOONLIGHT ON THE RANGE (Spectrum, 1937), where Scott plays a dual role. The weakest was Fuzzy's last picture with Scott, SONGS AND BULLETS (Spectrum, 1938). After Fuzzy was replaced in the Scott series, Harry Harvey (fake beard and all) was brought in for Scott's sidekick. He was even billed as Fuzzy. But he was no Fuzzy St. John. And, he wasn't funny – he was pathetic.

Lois January commented at one of the film festivals about making MOONLIGHT ON THE RANGE (Spectrum, 1937): "Although cheaply and sloppily done, MOONLIGHT ON THE RANGE was one of my favorite pictures. After all this time, I remember it well. One reason it is a favorite is because I got to sing. Fred Scott was such wonderful gentleman. Of course, Fuzzy St. John was a dear. We all loved him."

FILMS WITH FRED SCOTT

(All made for Spectrum)
MELODY OF THE PLAINS (1937)
THE FIGHTING DEPUTY (1937)
MOONLIGHT ON THE RANGE (1937)
THE ROAMING COWBOY (1937)
THE RANGER'S ROUND-UP (1938)
KNIGHT OF THE PLAINS (1938)
SONGS AND BULLETS (1938)

Italian one sheet of Fred Scott and Fuzzy in KNIGHT OF THE PLAINS (Spectrum. 1938).

FILMS WITH DON "RED" BARRY

When film fans think of St. John, they naturally think of the movies he made for PRC. However, the finest of all the Western series that he participated in was not at PRC, but the six movies he made with Don Barry at Republic – although St. John was not always in a sidekick role. He was not called Fuzzy in any of the Barry features. Below is a list of St. John's films with Barry, followed by his character name.

(All Republic)
TEXAS TERRORS (1940) – Frosty Larsen
THE APACHE KID (1941) – Dangle
A MISSOURI OUTLAW (1941) – Dan Willoughby
STAGECOACH EXPRESS (1942) – Dusty Jenkins
ARIZONA TERRORS (1942) – Hardtack
JESSE JAMES, JR. (aka SUNDOWN FURY – Pop Sawyer)

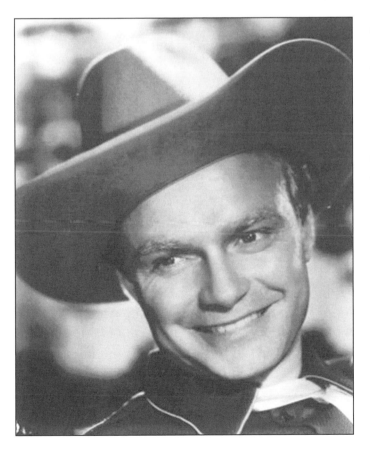

All the films with Barry are quite entertaining. Perhaps the best is JESSE JAMES, JR. due to Fuzzy's fancy bike riding. Fuzzy rides his bike backwards into a saloon, and comes out riding the bike with a beer in one hand. He then tosses the empty glass back into the saloon and rides on. Next, he rides the bike up to a picket fence, and goes over the handle bars and over the fence. There are also several other scenes with Fuzzy and his bike.

In the film, Fuzzy owns a livery stable but, due to being allergic to horses, he has to wear a protective mask while working with the animals.

Of all the films in which Fuzzy appeared, this may be the one that showcased him the best.

The weakest of the Barry pictures is A MISSOURI OUTLAW (Republic, 1941) because Fuzzy is so subdued and not his usual boisterous self.

(Note: "Doc" Tommy Scott, whom Fuzzy later made personal appearances with after his film career, recalls one of Fuzzy's bicycle tricks: "He tightened the handle bars where he could turn them a bit to the left and the bicycle would stay there. He would ride out on stage and, just at the right moment, jump off and send the bicycle rolling away from him at a pretty good speed. He had the bicycle set so it would make a turn automatically and started back towards him. When the bicycle was a few feet away from him, he would whistle, start making hand motions, and say, "Come here bicycle" in his most coaxing voice, and then jump back on it and ride away. It got the audience laughing every time.")

(Note: On July 17, 1980, Barry and his wife Barbara got into a fight. Barry tried to strangle her, but she managed to escape. Don was screaming all the while, "Don't leave me Barbara – I'll kill myself." The police were called to the scene to stop the altercation. Thinking they had things under control, the officers headed back to their car. Barry, then, came rushing out of the house wielding a .38 caliber revolver. He shot himself in the head before the officers could get back to him and died on the way to the hospital.

According to his former wife, Peggy Stewart, Barry had been on Valium for about a year, and, although not a drinker, he did enjoy wine. He drank a glass of wine on the afternoon of his death. She suspects the mixture of wine, with the Valium, might have caused his irrational behavior.)

THE LONE RIDER MOVIES

The Lone Ranger serials from Republic in 1938 and 1939 had proven very popular and PRC, by offering The Lone Rider series, was obviously out to confuse viewers into thinking they were going to see a Lone Ranger film. The studio teamed Fuzzy with George Houston for the initial Lone Rider pictures, but the films certainly were no prize-winners, and Fuzzy definitely outshone the rigid star. One of Fuzzy's shining moments is in THE LONE RIDER IN CHEYENNE (PRC, 1942) where his attempt at threading a needle gives a lot of chuckles. Fuzzy had initially played with Houston in FRONTIER SCOUT (Grand National, 1938). Houston must have been dull even to those with whom he worked because Beth Marion, his leading lady in FRONTIER SCOUT, said, "I've seen stills and lobby cards of FRONTIER SCOUT featuring George Houston and myself but, for the life of me, I don't remember George Houston."

(Note: It had been publicized that Houston would make eight Billy the Kid films in 1940, but the studio changed its mind.)

Don Miller, in *Hollywood Corral,* wrote: "It takes no great deduction to state PRC was earnestly hoping for a Lone Ranger/Lone Rider similarity to present itself to the youngsters, but Houston didn't use any of the flamboyant gimmickry connected to the masked rider."

(Note: Bob Livingston confirmed that having him don a mask was a feeble attempt by PRC to capitalize on Livingston's popularity as the Lone Ranger in Republic's 1939 serial THE LONE RANGER RIDES AGAIN.)

It's hard to pick the best of the Houston/Fuzzy pictures because none were very good. Perhaps THE LONE RIDER AMBUSHED (PRC, 1941), where Houston plays a double role should get the nod as the best while OUTLAWS OF BOULDER PASS (PRC, 1942), the last in the series, is the worst. Houston, like Fred Scott, was no actor, and, like Scott, his operatic singing did not appeal to the younger viewers.

(Note: George Houston died under unusual circumstances. In 1944, a few years after his film career, he was on his usual walk along Franklin Avenue in Hollywood when he was stricken with a heart attack. The police came upon George lying on the sidewalk; thinking he was drunk they brought him to headquarters and detained him in the Drunk Tank. This, his family members believe, hastened his demise. The newspaper reported, "Actor Dies in Police Custody.")

After Houston's departure from PRC, Bob Livingston was brought in for The Lone Rider pictures, and Fuzzy continued in the sidekick role. Livingston was a logical choice since he wasn't doing anything after leaving the Three Mesquiteers series, and he had played the Lone Ranger.

While not outstanding, the Livingston/St. John PRC features were good or better than anything else put out by PRC. Livingston could act, and both men were experienced pros and pleasing to watch. The talent of the two veteran actors complemented each other. Livingston, who disliked many with whom he worked, had no problems with Fuzzy and said, "He was always on stage, whether he was on camera or not. We got along great." LAW OF THE SADDLE (PRC, 1943) and RAIDERS OF RED GAP (PRC, 1943) were the best films in the series, while DEATH RIDES THE PLAINS (PRC, 1943) WILD HORSE RUSTLERS (PRC, 1943) were the worst. The latter is a one of the many WWII propaganda films turned out by Hollywood in the 1940s. In this picture, Nazis slip into the U.S. to kill horses intended for the U. S. Cavalry. The film was bad then and even worse today because it is so badly dated.

Merrill McCord, in his great book *Brothers of the West*, wrote of the series: "The reason why the Livingston/St. John films rate near the top of C-Westerns (a step below the B-Westerns) was the stars themselves. Each had acting skills, personality, charisma, and an attitude to make mediocre products look good. Rapport between Livingston and St. John was apparent in the beginning, and grew with each film.

"Livingston clowned around more in this series than any of his other Western series. He and St. John at times looked like a polished comedy team, as they played off each other and seemed to enjoy it. St. John virtually had an equal role with the star in the pictures. He often upstaged Livingston, who evidently did not mind. Reviewers often took note of St. John's scene-stealing in the series."

FILMS WITH GEORGE HOUSTON

(Houston as "Tom Cameron")
(All PRC)

THE LONE RIDER RIDES ON (1941)
THE LONE RIDER CROSSES THE RIO (1941)
THE LONE RIDER IN GHOST TOWN (1941)
THE LONE RIDER IN FRONTIER FURY (1941)
THE LONE RIDER AMBUSHED (1941)
THE LONE RIDER FIGHTS BACK (1941) (with Dennis Moore in a non-Smoky role)
THE LONE RIDER AND THE BANDIT (1942) (with Dennis Moore)
THE LONE RIDER IN CHEYENNE (1942) (with Dennis Moore)
TEXAS JUSTICE (1942) (with Dennis Moore)
THE LONE RIDER IN BORDER ROUNDUP (1942) (with Dennis Moore)
OUTLAWS OF BOULDER PASS (1942) (with Dennis Moore)

FILMS WITH BOB LIVINGSTON

(Livingston initially plays "Tom Cameron," and then "Rocky Cameron")
(All PRC)
OVERLAND STAGECOACH (1942) (also with Dennis Moore)
DEATH RIDES THE PLAINS (1943)
WILD HORSE RUSTLERS (1943)
WOLVES ON THE RANGE (1943)
LAW OF THE SADDLE (1943)
RAIDERS OF RED GAP (1943)

(Note: Livingston played Rocky Cameron in some of the films. In 1944 Gene Alsace (aka Buck Coburn) assumed a similar name, Rocky Camron - without an "e.)

BILLY THE KID FILMS

(All PRC)

Fuzzy continued his merry ways in the PRC *Billy the Kid* series with Bob Steele until Steele was offered a better deal ($1,250 a picture) at Republic for some Three Mesquiteers films. Buster Crabbe then stepped into the part as the new Billy the Kid, which changed to Billy Carson starting with THE DEVIL RIDERS (1943), with Fuzzy remaining in the sidekick role. Other than Livingston and Steele, Crabbe was the best actor of the leading cowboy stars with whom Fuzzy sidekicked.

Steele and St. John were not strangers because, as mentioned earlier, Fuzzy had appeared with Steele in THE OKLAHOMA CYCLONE and THE LAND OF MISSING MEN, both 1930 Tiffany films, and in RIDERS OF THE DESERT (World Wide, 1932).

(Note: Bob Steele "sang" in the 1930 THE OKLAHOMA CYCLONE movie. Supposedly, it made him one of the first, if not the first, singing cowboys. But Steele, like John Wayne, was dubbed by Steele's brother William Bradbury. Wayne was also dubbed in a film by movie heavy Jack Kirk. Steele commented, "My dad used my twin brother Bill to dub Duke in RIDERS OF DESTINY (Monogram, 1933), as he had done several times in the past to dub me in a couple of films, as Bill could at least stay on key and carry a tune, and I could do neither, and the small fee Bill got helped to pay his bills in medical school.")

In the initial PRC *Billy the Kid* pictures, Bob Steele and Fuzzy were assisted by Carleton Young (Rex Lease subbed for Young in one film). When Crabbe took over the role, PRC continued the trio approach for about a half-dozen films before Buster and Fuzzy went on their own as a duo. In that half-dozen, the third member was most often Dave O'Brien, but Carleton Young and Bud McTaggart was the third member in one film each. The best of the Steeles was BILLY THE KID OUTLAWED (PRC, 1940). The worst was BILLY THE KID'S GUN JUSTICE (PRC, 1940).

(Note: Malcolm "Bud" McTaggart died in a swimming pool accident on May 29, 1949, just six days short of his 39th birthday. At one time, he was married to actress Pamela Blake.)

At a Memphis Film Festival, Bob Steele talked about working with Fuzzy: "Al and I weren't bosom buddies or anything like that, but I liked him, and I think he liked me. He had been around Hollywood almost since the beginning of moving pictures. We did our jobs and then went our separate ways. I enjoyed working with Al because he was a fine actor, and he was about my size."

BILLY THE KID MOVIES

(with Bob Steele)
BILLY THE KID OUTLAWED (1940)
BILLY THE KID IN TEXAS (1940)
BILLY THE KID'S GUN JUSTICE (1940)
BILLY THE KID'S RANGE WAR (1941)
BILLY THE KID'S FIGHTING PALS (1941)
BILLY THE KID IN SANTA FE (1941)

"Wait a minute, Fuzz. Let me take him."

BUSTER AND FUZZY

(From various articles and David Rothel's excellent book, *Those Great Cowboy Sidekicks*)

After Bob Steele stayed on at Republic for his second season 1941-42 of The Three Mesquiteers series, PRC hired Buster Crabbe for the Billy the Kid pictures. It was a smart move because Crabbe had great name recognition due to his roles in the Tarzan, Flash Gordon, and Buck Rogers serials.

All together, Crabbe and St. John made 36 Westerns all directed by Sam Newfield, hiding behind his Sherman Scott identity. Crabbe and St. John really meshed as a duo. Generally, the plots focused on Billy being charged with something he didn't do, and Crabbe (as Billy) is trying to prove the charges false. Later, the Billy the Kid name would be dropped in favor of Billy Carson.

By 1944 PRC thought St. John was now popular enough with Western film fans to use his screen name in a title (FUZZY SETTLES DOWN). It is the only time a cowboy sidekick's character name was featured in a title. Even Gabby Hayes and Smiley Burnette were not so honored.

Probably the best of the Buster Crabbe movies were GANGSTER'S DEN (PRC, 1945) and HIS BROTHER'S GHOST (PRC, 1945). In HIS BROTHER'S GHOST, Fuzzy steals the film as he plays a dual role by playing Fuzzy and Fuzzy's twin brother Andy. He is excellent all the way through. The worst entry has to be FRONTIER OUTLAWS (PRC, 1944) where, in one scene, Crabbe clearly bangs his head as he backs out of a window. Cheap PRC did not bother to reshoot the scene. To make matters worse, Crabbe uses an awful Mexican accent later in the film. In addition to Fuzzy's strong roles in HIS BROTHER'S GHOST and in FUZZY SETTLES DOWN, he also steals the show in BLAZING FRONTIERS (PRC, 1943).

(Note: PRC had such a reputation for making shoddy Westerns that Art Davis (a member of PRC's short-lived Frontier Marshals series

in 1942) jokingly stated that PRC stood for "Pretty Rotten Crap." Actually, it stood for Producer's Releasing Corporation.)

Don Miller, in *Hollywood Corral*, wrote about the Crabbe/St. John series: "Crabbe was coasting in his hero role, but his easygoing manner combined with genuine acting skill made it look good. St. John had honed his Fuzzy character to a sharp point. Mugging, pratfalls, anything, and everything went into the role. With trousers at crotch level and stubbled chin perpetually outthrust, he presented the picture of a Western court jester. He had developed a bit of business that would never fail – the ludicrous bravado as he slithered off his horse while eyeing a potential enemy, or his reaction to a knockout blow, an unconcerned wide grin as if to say it didn't hurt a bit, followed by total collapse. Then there was his rubber-legged comic routine to show how frightened he was."

Perhaps Les Adams and Buck Rainey offered the best description of the Crabbe/St. John films in their book, *Shoot-Em-Ups*: "The Buster Crabbe – Al St. John series was PRC's most popular one, and it was in production through the Golden Years. Although cheaply made, like the other PRC features, these films were usually enjoyable. Crabbe and St. John made a good team, and Charles King and Kermit Maynard were usually in the supporting lineup, which was a plus factor for discriminating buffs. Appeal was primarily to the rural and the kiddie audience, and bookings were usually restricted to second and third rate houses. Buster was simply not given a chance to rise above mediocrity in his PRC films. Credit is due to both Crabbe and St. John for their personal popularity when evaluating the success of their Western series, for every aspect of production and story was poor. Suffice it to say that none of the films ever won an Academy Award for anything or even honorable mention. But they were horse operas, and their effulgence lay in the fact that Buster was tough and implacable. Al St. John was funny, the girls stayed pretty much out of the way, and the outlaws were familiar and predictable."

BUSTER CRABBE TALKS

"My co-star for the Billy the Kid series was Fuzzy St. John, who I'd watched as a youngster in the Al St. John comedy series in movies, so that seemed like a plus to me.

"Fuzzy was the greatest. Every once in a while he'd ride a bike in one of our Westerns. We'd work in some way so he could be on it. He could really ride a bike well – spin the front wheels and ride on the back wheels, ride on the handle bars, or whatever. He created much of his own comedy, like coming out of a swing saloon door and stumbling, or falling down stairs and that type of thing.

"After we signed with PRC for the series, we went out to a San Fernando Valley ranch where many of the movie horses were stabled. There were several ranches around town that supplied horses to studios, so we had our pick of the available stock. Since I was to star in the series, the horse I selected would be reserved for my exclusive use, and it had to be of sufficient quality and appearance to befit my heroic image. I tried several, wanting one with enough gumption to take my lead easily and not kick me to Chatsworth every time I walked behind it. Also, I wanted one with an easy gait, comfortable to ride. I settled on a sturdy palomino named Falcon, with a white blaze on its nose and forehead. Fuzzy ended up with a white-nosed chestnut, a good looking animal that showed up dark on the screen to highlight Falcon. After being fitted with saddles and tack, we rode around the ranch for a few hours to get used to the animals.

"The studio supplied us with our basic costumes. I wore a light-colored hat with a jaw strap affixed to it. I never liked having my hat blow off my head when riding a horse. Fuzzy stayed in character, too. He was dressed in a scroungy plaid shirt, ragged vest, dirty, baggy jeans, suspenders, and a ragged hat. It was all arranged rather haphazardly around his face full of whiskers. Fuzzy and I worked well together to the point where we could anticipate each other's moves and styles and adlib some of our lines whenever the mood struck us. Fuzzy was always good for a good belly laugh. He pulled us out a lot of times by doing his funny thing. We worked well together because we got to know how each other worked.

"Fuzzy had a lot of funny battles with Charlie King. He would work out a routine between them for those comic fights – funny, really funny. And when things went wrong, it was even funnier – when one of them miscued or something like that.

"Most people know Fuzzy had a drinking problem. I had to keep an eye on him and drag him out of places. Once, we were walking down the street to a theater for a performance when I turned around and found out I had been talking to myself. We'd just passed a bar. I retraced my steps, and sure enough, there was Fuzzy holding court at the bar with a lot of people gathered around him. Flo (Fuzzy's wife) had a job keeping an eye on old Fuzz. He was always in some kinda trouble. He really had a drinking problem.

"Now, I don't mean to belittle the talents of the comics in the B-Westerns. They were, on the whole, some pretty good actors who carried a lot of the burden in the pictures. Their being cast as louts was part of the mode of the day. Raymond Hatton, Fuzzy Knight, Al St. John, and Smiley Burnette were just a few of the sidekicks who had tremendous talent. In some instances, they might well have been the best actors in the movie. I think without a doubt that Fuzzy was far and away the best of all the Western comics. That includes Gabby Hayes, Andy Devine, Smiley Burnette, and Fuzzy Knight.

"It was only many years after my series that I learned that Bob Steele had made some Billy the Kid Westerns. Sig Newfield and his brother Sam directed the pictures that Fuzzy and I made for PRC. I don't know what the production costs for our picture were but I would guess around $20,000. I was paid $1,000, and I think Fuzzy was paid about the same.

"We didn't let ourselves get carried away with pranks. Fuzz would perform slapstick stuff, because he was a natural clown. If his part called for doltishness, he'd milk it for all it was worth. He wasn't any more thrilled with some of the products we turned out than was I, but he was an excellent actor and a great guy. He used a lot of his slapstick to ease his own frustrations. Like me, he knew there was no way we could make a silk purse out of a sow's ear. If the producers didn't take our films seriously, there wasn't much point in the actors getting uptight over them.

"I finally quit due to the lack of decent scripts and cuts in productions. Believe it or not, we started the last "Billy" film on Monday and wrapped it up on Thursday. The next day I quit. They didn't even bat an eye; they just brought in Lash LaRue.

"Some say my acting rose to the level of incompetence and then leveled off. I was a lot better actor than people gave me credit for. I didn't have any training, but I feel if I had been given the chance, I could have become a really good, top-rate actor. I didn't make it like a Gable or Boyer. But I wonder what would have happened if things had been different.

"When we weren't working, Fuzzy and I visited the soldiers at mess halls and canteens on base, chatting with homesick men who were anxious about where they'd be sent and what the future held for them.

"The war effort took many budding actors and established stars away from Hollywood for a while, and those with families were channeled into USO activity and propaganda films as well as military-training documentaries. Since I was 34 years old in 1942 and deferrable because of my family status, Fuzzy and I joined a photographic unit out of the Hal Roach Studio to make instruction films for the field artillery.

"One of the places we visited was Fort Sill, Oklahoma. Many of the young men at Fort Sill were fans of ours, having seen our movies and the Flash Gordon serials as teenagers, so I was often introduced as Flash Gordon or Tarzan, as well as Billy the Kid, in addition to my actual name."

In the book *Buster Crabbe: A Self-Portrait*, by Kark Whitezel, Buster told the following story about how Fuzzy Knight was cast in "Captain Gallant of the Foreign Legion": "Harry Salzman (the producer) asked me who I'd like to have for the sidekick in the series. Since I'd always worked well with Al "Fuzzy" St. John, I suggested that, if the old Western association didn't get in the way, Fuzzy would be nice for a partner. We had worked together in 36 films, so I took it for granted the advertising executives who were putting the television package together knew about Fuzzy's identification with me. Salzman said he'd see if Fuzzy could be signed, and the matter was dropped. Soon, I got a call from Salzman telling me Fuzzy would be in New York the following day. I agreed to come to the office at that time so the contracts could be finalized.

"When I walked into Salzman's large office, I saw instantly that a mistake had been made. The actor sitting in a chair talking to some men wasn't Fuzzy St. John. It was Fuzzy Knight, a venerable sidekick to many cowboy stars, but never to me. We had worked together in two films, TO THE LAST MAN in 1933 and SHE HAD TO CHOOSE in 1934. I called Salzman to one side. 'I didn't mean Fuzzy Knight. I was talking about Fuzzy St. John.'

"'I'm sorry, Buster. When you said 'Fuzzy,' we put out a call for a 'Fuzzy,' and he's what we came up with."

"I couldn't help but wonder, if they had given the role to Roy Rogers, would the executives have hired Gabby Hartnett (a professional baseball great) instead of Hayes?

'Can he handle the part?' I asked. 'He's available and he's agreed to sign.'

"It's been rumored around Hollywood that he has a drinking problem, serious enough to affect his work.'

'I know, but Mr. Knight has put our minds at ease on that. He's been on the wagon for several years now. I believe him and if it's okay with you, I think he'll be good in the part.'

"I had nothing against Fuzzy Knight, and I already regretted making such a big deal out of it. To amend the error might have caused harm to Fuzzy while, as it stood, Al St. John was no worse off for not ever knowing he was in the running. For all I knew, the job would be a lift for Fuzzy Knight, and it wasn't my place to pass judgment on the man. I told Harry I had no objections, and walked across the room extending my hand to Fuzzy. He greeted me with a smile and began chuckling words at me in that characteristic out-of-the-side-of-his-mouth fashion of his. Anyway, I was pleased to work with Fuzzy Knight. Both Fuzzys were great guys and delightful to work with."

(Note: At times, Crabbe told a different story about Fuzzy Knight getting the TV role: "When we were looking for a fellow to play my sidekick in the 'Captain Gallant of the Foreign Legion' TV series, I told the producer to look up Al "Fuzzy" St. John. When he contacted Fuzzy, poor old Fuzzy was loaded. They signed Fuzzy Knight. Knight had once had a drinking problem, too. But I surely admired his work in pictures and was glad to have him on my TV series."

It is rather strange in that Fuzzy Knight was originally chosen for Fred Scott's sidekick but the role went to Fuzzy St. John. Then Crabbe suggested Fuzzy St. John for the role in his TV series, but it was Fuzzy Knight who got the job.)

"Save me, Buster."

"You can bet Sleazy Stan Jolley is up to no good."

John Brooker called Joel Newfield at his California home in November 2009 and asked him if he had any memories about working with Fuzzy in the Buster Crabbe westerns Billy the Kid Wanted and Billy the Kid's Smoking Guns in 1941-42.

Newfield responded, "My goodness that's a long, long time ago, I was pretty young at the time - about 6 or 7. My dad was the director. They were the cheapest made movies, and he worked on two a week They got down to pennies on those film, it was amazing, He threw me in them just for fun. At that time everyone went to the Saturday matinees to see Fuzzy because he was very popular. Gabby Hayes and Fuzzy were the two most popular sidekicks with us kids. Fuzzy was very entertaining on set and we had a couple of scenes together. I remember one scene in a kitchen where he lifted me up and sat me on a shelf or something and he did some cooking, and there was an explosion. I think I ended up with a saucepan on my head. He was kind of quiet, so I don't remember him as a person…. I seem to remember hearing talk that he was a drinker. later on I heard he was traveling around with a circus. I've seen the movies on TV now and then. My family sometimes send me posters or pictures they've picked up from those movies"

Little Joel Newfield is pictured with Buster, Fuzzy, Dave O'Brien, and Choto Sherwood in (BILLY THE KID WANTED, PRC 1941). *(Note: It was Choto Sherwood's only screen appearance.)*

BILLY THE KID/BILLY CARSON FILMS

(with Buster Crabbe)

(13 Films with Buster Crabbe as "Billy the Kid")

BILLY THE KID WANTED (1941)
BILLY THE KID'S ROUND-UP (1941)
BILLY THE KID TRAPPED (1942)
BILLY THE KID'S SMOKING GUNS (1942)
LAW AND ORDER (1942) (Dual role for Crabbe as Billy the Kid and Lt. Ted Morrison)
SHERIFF OF SAGE VALLEY (1942) (Dual role for Buster as Billy & Kansas Ed Bonney)
THE MYSTERIOUS RIDER (1943)
THE KID RIDES AGAIN (1943)
FUGITIVE OF THE PLAINS (1943)
WESTERN CYCLONE (1943)
CATTLE STAMPEDE (1943)
THE RENEGADE (1943)
BLAZING FRONTIER (1943)

(23 Films with Buster Crabbe as "Billy Carson")

THE DEVIL RIDERS (1943)
FRONTIER OUTLAWS (1944)
VALLEY OF VENGEANCE (1944)
THE DRIFTER (1944) (Dual role for Buster as Billy Carson and Drifter Davis)
RUSTLERS' HIDEOUT (1944)
WILD HORSE PHANTOM (1944)
OATH OF VENGEANCE (1944)
THUNDERING GUNSLINGERS (1944)
FUZZY SETTLES DOWN (1944)
HIS BROTHER'S GHOST (1945) (Dual role for St. John as Fuzzy Jones and Andy Jones)
SHADOWS OF DEATH (1945)
GANGSTER'S DEN (1945)
STAGECOACH OUTLAWS (1945)
BORDER BADMEN (1945)
FIGHTING BILL CARSON (1945)
PRAIRIE RUSTLERS (1945) (Dual role for Buster as Billy Carson and Jim Slade)
LIGHTNING RAIDERS (1946)

TERRORS ON HORSEBACK (1946)
GENTLEMEN WITH GUNS (1946)
GHOST OF HIDDEN VALLEY (1946)
PRAIRIE BADMEN (1946)
OVERLAND RIDERS (1946)
OUTLAWS OF THE PLAINS (1946)

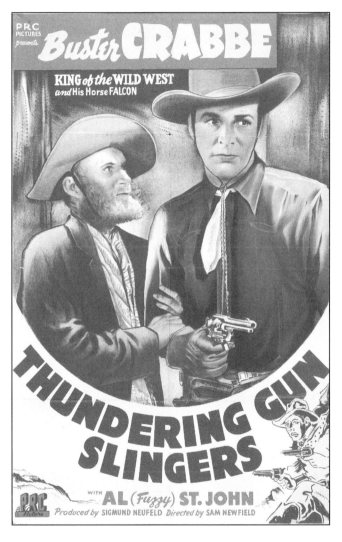

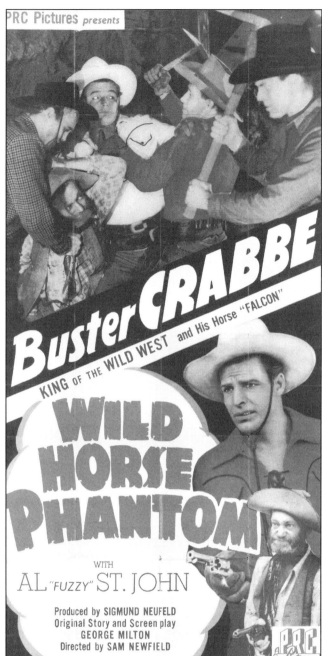

LASH AND FUZZY

Thanks in part to David Rothel for allowing me to use quotes from two of his books: *Lash LaRue – King of the Bullwhip* and *Those Great Cowboy Sidekicks* (my favorite cowboy book). Many of the comments from Lash came from the various film festivals that he attended.

The Lash LaRue/Fuzzy films, although they made an impact on the public, were no more than average B-Westerns (many far below average). LaRue was no actor. Some regard Lash as only a co-star because the outrageously funny St. John contributed as much, or more, to the success of the series as did LaRue.

Don Miller, in *Hollywood Corral*, wrote of the first entry DEAD MAN'S GOLD (Western Adventure/Screen Guild), which the same could be said for many of the LaRue/St. John features: "The film consists of practically no plot, scant dialogue, but much riding around, punctuated by loud bursts of action. To give the riding scenes more adrenalin, composer Walter Greene had his orchestra playing at fever pitch, even though nothing was occurring on the screen at the moment. It was noisy enough to keep the patrons awake, and made the action all the more welcome when it came."

Some gimmicks that Fuzzy used were sure to get some laughs: When involved in a fight scene, he would often wrap his legs around the badguy's waist, and pulls the villain's hat down over his eyes while continuing to pound away at his opponent with both fists. It was always funny when he was the recipient of a haymaker by one of the heavies in a bar room fight, then give big smile before sliding down the front the bar as he went into unconsciousness. And when he rolled a cigarette, often with one hand, it was sure to bring a giggle from the audience. Of course, Fuzzy was always the brave one – as long as he knew the hero was close by to handle the rough stuff.

Of all the cowboy heroes Fuzzy sidekicked with, the best chemistry was with Buster Crabbe. It was obvious they were fond of one another. Crabbe, like Bob Livingston had done, would playfully laugh and poke at him – whereas, Lash LaRue seldom did. Crabbe often just called him "Fuzz," as if he was a dear friend. But Crabbe sometimes went overboard in his laughter over Fuzzy's zany antics.

In quite a few of these downright poverty-stricken pictures, St. John provided the only glimmer of entertainment. Fuzzy became extremely popular with the young movie-goers. He was unique among cowboy sidekicks in that more than often he actually carried the films rather than the leading men. In other words, people often were as interested in seeing Fuzzy as they

were Buster Crabbe or Lash LaRue. Both Crabbe and LaRue were well aware of this and remained steadfast in their praise of the diminutive performer.

When B-Westerns bit the dust in the early 1950s, Fuzzy teamed with LaRue for awhile and traveled with Royal American Shows playing state fairs. Later, he and Lash made appearances at movie houses across the country or anywhere that they could make a few bucks.

In 1957, while appearing at the Mid-South Fair in Memphis, Tennessee, police arrested Lash and Fuzzy, and charged them with the possession of stolen property. It seems someone had offered Lash a deal he couldn't refuse on some stolen sewing machines. The case against Fuzzy was dropped, and a jury acquitted Lash. Upon hearing the verdict, Lash cried.

When Lash's personal life hit the skids, Fuzzy would make appearances alone – usually in worn-out theaters in small towns.

(Note: I met Fuzzy in my hometown (Oak Ridge, Tennessee) around 1950. He was alone. I do not recall a great deal about his show except for him reaching out his hand like he was leaning against a walk and then intentionally falling to the floor – as if the make-believe wall had moved. He would also bounce around on stage, let his legs collapse, and then spring up again before hitting the floor. He fired a few shots before his pistol jammed. After the show, I asked him to autograph a small piece of paper I had with me. He only signed it "Fuzzy." I did not find him very friendly, but, in fairness to him, he was still trying to get his pistol unjammed when I interrupted him for the autograph.)

The best of the LaRue series were OUTLAW COUNTRY (Western Ad-

Fuzzy and Lash at the 1957 Mid-South Fair in Memphis.

venture/Screen Guild, 1949), GHOST TOWN RENEGADES (PRC, 1947), and KING OF THE BULLWHIP (Western Adventure, 1951), the latter primarily due to the outstanding cast.

The absolute worst of the LaRue pictures was the ridiculous and shoddy THE DALTONS' WOMEN (Western Adventure, 1951), closely followed by THE VANISHING OUTPOST (Western Adventure, 1951), THE BLACK LASH (Western Adventure, 1952) and THE FRONTIER PHANTOM (Western Adventure, 1952). The last three were composed of about 50 percent of stock footage.

Anne Gwynne talked about making KING OF THE BULLWHIP: "I did it for the money. Most of it was stock footage. There were quite a few old-timers in it – good people like Jack Holt, Michael Whalen, Tom Neal, and Dennis Moore, but it wasn't much of a picture, far below the quality of pictures I had experienced earlier."

Exhibitors also loved Fuzzy because he could be counted on to attract moviegoers. The Fuzzy character was the main box-office draw in these films when they were shown in England and Europe. In fact, in Germany the film titles always featured Fuzzy, rather than whatever cowboy hero he was paired with.

(Note: Lash liked to tell the story of how two German fans came over to his table at a personal appearance and began speaking to him in German. Lash told them that he could not speak German, and one fan said in surprised voice, "Oh, of course you can, we saw all of your movies, and you and Fuzzy spoke German very well." The two fans obviously did not realize that American-made movies had voices dubbed for showing in foreign lands.)

Lash LaRue: "Fuzzy and Buster had been close friends. One day about six months after Fuzzy and I began to work together, he walked up to me and said, "You know, I wasn't going to like you, but you are all right."

"Fuzzy was a wonderful friend and a good teacher. I learned a lot from him. God must have put me with him so I could learn. He was a fantastic acrobat. He was like a piece of spring steel. He used to think of Fuzzy as a separate character from himself. He would think of something funny and say, 'That would be cute for Fuzzy to do.' That's a wonderful way to separate yourself from your show career.

"Fuzzy had a bad drinking problem. The bottle had him pretty bad. I couldn't understand why he wouldn't stop drinking. Then I met his wife, and I understood. She would cause anyone to drink. She was a hypochondriac who went all over the country looking for a doctor who wanted to operate. Fuzzy's important dialogue had to be shot in the morning because during lunch break, someone would slip him a drink and he'd begin to mumble. He was an alcoholic who couldn't handle two or three drinks at lunch time.

(Note: St. John was not the only sidekick to have a bout with the bottle. Others, who at times drank to excess, include Pat Brady, Dub Taylor, Fuzzy Knight, Emmett Lynn, Lasses White, Wally Vernon, Raymond Hatton, and Pat Buttram. Smiley Burnette did not drink, and Gabby Hayes enjoyed a glass of wine.)

"Fuzzy did not have a very happy home life. In fact, he couldn't even sign his check from the studio. He had to sign it and give it to his wife. The check was made out to him and to her. She was more of a keeper than a wife. When she died, I guess he thought he had to have someone to tell him what to do so, he married again. And the woman kept him working the rest of his life.

"I think this wife married him to get on the stage herself. She was one of those performers that played the glasses – you know, they fill each glass with a different level of water and then play a tune. She'd go out and book Fuzzy on personal appearances, and then she'd come along and do her act. *(Note: Someone else said she played tunes on a set of bells.)*

"Fuzzy was an angel unaware. He didn't understand the whole story of the life and death and monopoly of the soul, but he was a beautiful person. Fuzzy was just Fuzzy, you couldn't duplicate him even if you tried. I don't really think of him as being gone; the spirit of him will be here forever. He was a sweet guy. He was just a lonesome guy that looked all his life for love and never really found it."

(Note: LaRue talked very little about his early life, but did say he was born Alfred LaRue in Gretna, Louisiana. Yet, his death certificate lists his birthplace as Michigan and his father's name as Wilson. If Lash had used his real surname, Roland Charles Meyers may have never become Whip Wilson.)

Peggy Stewart recalled working in three Western Adventure films (THE BLACK LASH (1952), DEAD MAN'S GOLD (1948), and FRONTIER REVENGE (1948) with Lash and Fuzzy: "It was quite different working for Ron Ormond than it was working for Republic. Lash did not look like a cowboy. I had not seen any of his pictures when I started working with him. When I first looked at him, I wondered if he could even ride. He looked like he should have been in other types of films. But he knew his dialogue, and gave an excellent reading.

"He and Fuzzy worked so well together; they were a team. I loved watching Fuzzy work with Lash. It was plain to see that they cared a lot for each other. To hear Lash talk about Fuzzy at the festivals over the years, it is obvious that he loved him very much.

"Lash would listen to things Fuzzy would say. And he and Ron Ormond would then talk it over and get a lot of it in the picture. Ron had control over directing Lash and Fuzzy even off the set. He set up most of their road-show tours. He kept them busy on the road between pictures. I thought Lash was a good actor and underrated. I think he should have gone further. Lash would have made a good character actor."

Once again, Fuzzy had been in series of poor-to-fair films, and once again with an actor who could not act. Les Adams and Buck Rainey wrote about the series in Shoot-Em-Ups: "LaRue was a whip-cracking, obstreperous, black-garbed, sulky, gangster-looking, tough-talking poor specimen who never should have been cast in a lead. His success was a quirk. He was as unbelievably bad as an actor that often people were drawn to him either in sympathy or in disbelief that such a cowboy could be filling the screen once occupied by Buck Jones, Ken Maynard, and George O'Brien. Perhaps audiences came to see the loveable, scene-stealing little guy who shared co-starring honors – Al St. John, who was consistently picking fights for his partner to finish."

Fuzzy commented on his career: "I've been around for a long time, and worked with a lot of good cowboys. I had fun, and they treated me swell. There was never a problem. I guess I enjoyed working with Buster the most. We worked well together, and he appreciated me. I think we had about equal screen time and made about the same amount of money. When Buster left the series, they brought in Lash LaRue to replace him. Lash and I got along just fine. We made a lot of personal appearances together."

(Regarding the potential success of one of his films): "There's no way of telling. It's sorta like an unborn baby. With films, you never know how until it comes out of the cutting room and goes on the screen."

In the late 1950s, Fuzzy joined up with the famous "Doc" Tommy Scott Medicine Show as a featured attraction. He was among several former stars that Scott used in his show which included Johnny Mack Brown, Tim McCoy, and Sunset Carson. Fuzzy performed his comedy act, and entertained on the show for about five years according to Scott.

Nearly everyone agrees that St. John's screen character name, Fuzzy Q. Jones, was as familiar to Western fans of that era as was William Boyd's as Hopalong Cassidy. In each instance, the actor was better known to the young audiences by the character he played rather than by his real name. In fact, it is doubtful that many of the youngsters could even identify the name Alfred St. John.

Fuzzy was an outrageously funny buffoon who shuffled and stumbled his way through so many Westerns at PRC that he became a fixture at the cheap studio. As Fuzzy Q. Jones, he provided us with many fun-filled Saturdays. A great deal of the PRC Westerns would not have been worth watching if it had not been for Fuzzy.

In an article in a 1970 issue of Deadwood Magazine, a writer wrote: "It isn't hard to conjure up once again the vision of that bewhiskered face with the impish grin; the wide mischievous eyes; the stuttering dialogue; and those outlandish clothes (several sizes too big). They all add up to one of the fondest memories of childhood – Al "Fuzzy" St. John."

THAT'S OUR FUZZY!!!

"Lash, we can clean up this town in short order."

Fuzzy, Lash, and Brad Slaven will settle this affair.

TIDBITS

(All films listed are PRC unless otherwise indicated)

Fuzzy's parents were Walter (born in Ohio) and Nora (born in Indiana). Both were in vaudeville. From 1912 to 1952, Fuzzy appeared in some 350 films – many were comedy shorts.

In the early days of silents, due to his small size, he often donned a dress and doubled women. Sam Newfield directed over 70 films in which Fuzzy participated.

Fuzzy did not work in any serials. However, in the 1948 Republic serial THE JAMES BROTHERS OF MISSOURI, Fuzzy can be seen in chapter 8 in stock footage taken from the Don "Red" Barry feature THE APACHE KID (Republic, 1941).

He did not use the name Fuzzy in the films with Barry.

In THE LONE RIDER RIDES ON (1941), Fuzzy joins George Houston in singing "Nobody's Fault But My Own."

He gets to warble "Calico Joe" in THE LONE RIDER IN GHOST TOWN (1941).

PRC must have liked Fuzzy's work because from 1940-1943 he appeared in the Billy the Kid films with Bob Steele and Buster Crabbe, in the Lone Rider series with George Houston and with Bob Livingston, and with the Frontier Marshals starring Lee Powell, Art Davis, and Bill "Cowboy Rambler" Boyd.

In OVERLAND STAGE COACH (1942), Fuzzy not only co-stars but also narrates the film.

Bob Livingston is billed as "Rocky Cameron" in WILD HORSE RUSTLERS (1943) and Fuzzy does calls him "Rocky" three times, but, on three other occasions, Lane Chandler calls him "Tom."

Dennis Moore joined George Houston and Fuzzy for six of the Lone Rider films, and Moore was in one The Lone Rider picture starring Bob Livingston and Fuzzy.

In the Steele/Fuzzy film BILLY THE KID'S RANGE WAR (1941), Steele calls his horse "Toby."

Fuzzy does his one-handed roll of a cigarette in THE LONE RIDER IN TEXAS JUSTICE (1942).

In Buster Crabbe's series with Fuzzy, Crabbe was billed as "King of the Wild West."

Crabbe rode a horse called Falcon.

Look for Fuzzy and his bike in Don Barry's JESSE JAMES, JR. aka SUNDOWN FURY (Republic, 1942.)

He rides his bike again in Crabbe's THE DRIFTER (1943).

He's back on the bike for some fancy riding with Crabbe's PRAIRIE RUSTLERS (1945).

In BORDER BADMEN (1945), Fuzzy has an inheritance from a 32nd cousin.

WILD HORSE PHANTOM (1944) incorporates the prop bat from PRC's 1941 highly successful horror movie THE DEVIL BAT, starring Bela Lugosi. The film is set in the 1880s but the PRC stock footage used for the prison escape contains 1940s automobiles, search lights, and weapons.

PRAIRIE RUSTLERS (1945) was budgeted at $22,500 and was shot in six days for $23,304.12. Star Buster Crabbe was paid $3,000; Fuzzy got $1,000.

Fuzzy slips and calls Crabbe "Bus" (instead of Billy) near the movie's end of PRAIRIE BADMEN (1946).

Fuzzy plays a dual role in HIS BROTHER'S GHOST (1945). The only other B-Western sidekick to play a dual role was Smiley Burnette in FIREBRANDS OF ARIZONA (Republic, 1944).

While working with Fuzzy, Buster Crabbe, Lash LaRue, George Houston, and Fred Scott played dual roles. Crabbe did it four times: LAW AND ORDER (1942), SHERIFF OF SAGE VALLEY (1942), THE DRIFTER (1943) and PRAIRIE RUSTLERS (1945). LaRue did it twice: OUTLAW COUNTRY (Western Adventure/Screen Guild, 1949) and FRONTIER PHANTOM (Western Adventure, 1952). Houston played a dual role in THE LONE RIDER AMBUSHED (1941). And Fred Scott did it once in MOONLIGHT ON THE RANGE (Spectrum, 1937).

Black Jack O'Shea, who is mostly uncredited in his some 200 films, gets to be the leader of the outlaw gang in LAW OF THE LASH (1947).

In MARK OF THE LASH (Western Adventure/Screen Guild, 1948) Fuzzy goofs and calls the girl lead "Suzi." Her real name was Suzi Crandall, but her character name was "Mary."

Add Fuzzy to the list of those who whipped up on Charlie King (CATTLE STAMPEDE (1943). And, in OUTLAWS OF THE PLAINS (1946), he gets to bulldog King off his horse. This was a rare event for a sidekick.

Incredibly, THE BLACK LASH (Western Adventure, 1952) with Lash and Fuzzy offers only about

15 minutes of new footage. The rest is from FRONTIER REVENGE (Western Adventure/Screen Guild, 1948). This was not the only LaRue picture to severely "cheat" the public.
Lash and Fuzzy made eight films together before LaRue is called "Lash." It first occurred in DEAD MAN'S GOLD (Western Adventure/Screen Guild, 1948).

Look for Fuzzy to do his fancy cigarette rolling in PIONEER JUSTICE (1947).

The Lash/Fuzzy movies, THE THUNDERING TRAIL (Western Adventure, 1951), and THE VANISHING OUTPOST (Western Adventure, 1951), also featured a girl named Sue Hussey. Ms. Hussey, who was from Alabama, only got the roles due to winning a contest. Both movies were probably shot at the same time. After that, Ms. Hussey was never heard from again.

(Note: Around 1992, I had Lash sign a lobby card from THE THUNDERING TRAIL, and he pointed to Hussey and told the story about her winning a contest to get cast in the picture.)

More than half of THE VANISHING OUTPOST (Western Adventure, 1951) consists of scenes cut from SON OF BILLY THE KID (Western Adventure/Screen Guild, 1949), SON OF A BADMAN (Western Adventure/Screen Guild, 1949), OUTLAW COUNTRY (Western Adventure/Screen Guild, 1949) and MARK OF THE LASH (Western Adventure/Screen Guild, 1948).

In THE VANISHING OUTPOST, Lash slugs a saloon thug (Archie Twitchell) in a barroom scene; the bad guy's hat falls off. But when we see him reeling from the punch against the wall, the hat has reappeared on his head.

Only five days were spent shooting KING OF THE BULLWHIP (Western Adventure, 1951).

Fuzzy ended his film career in LaRue's THE FRONTIER PHANTOM (Western Adventure, 1952).

Fuzzy's height was listed as 5-8 (doubtful he was that tall).

The name St. John is so rare that only 17 are listed at the Social Security Death Database. Apparently, Fuzzy's wife never filed for his death benefit with the Social Security Administration.

Fuzzy was cremated. His saddle pals George Houston, Fred Scott, Buster Crabbe, and Lash LaRue were also cremated.

He has a star on the Hollywood Walk of Fame at 6313 Hollywood Boulevard.

Some years after Fuzzy's death Duane Gilbert, of Frazer, Ohio, created the Fuzzy St. John Fan Club.

John "Lefty" Cason had better drop that gun.

Jennifer Holt, Lash, and Fuzzy.

FANS REMEMBER FUZZY

I have asked several knowledgeable film fans to express their views on Fuzzy and his place among the B-Western sidekicks. Some of the comments are sure to be a surprise.

Don Calhoun (provider of expert B-Western commentary for a PBS TV station): At times, Al "Fuzzy" St. John was a silent-movie sidekick cast in sound Westerns! I know, this conclusion is too obvious when you know about Fuzzy's background as a silent comedian. However, I was only 7 or 8 years old when I made this observation in discussions with my older brother and my dad about the best sidekicks. At that time, my vocabulary wasn't advanced enough to make the statement at the beginning of this article, but my argument was that Fuzzy didn't have to say a word to be funnier than the other sidekicks!

Fuzzy fascinated me with the way he got on and off his small horse, or the way he stepped off the wooden sidewalks, or his rubber-leg routine when he got hit on the head. His attempts to aid the heroes like Buster Crabbe, George Houston, Bob Steele, or other PRC Cowboys in fist fights brought on more hilarious physical feats by Fuzzy. His fall down antics never looked staged like those of Dub Taylor, Frank Mitchell, or Smiley Burnette. He didn't have to fall in a water trough, or take a pie in the face to force laughter. The more you saw Fuzzy, the more that you looked forward to seeing these moves in every picture.

Don't get me wrong! I also thought that Fuzzy was excellent with comedic dialogue and with situational humor. In my opinion, Fuzzy's golden years as a Western sidekick came in the Billy Carson films with Buster Crabbe in 1944 and 1945. The two pals developed an on-screen chemistry during the Billy the Kid phase of the series, and The Billy Carson films benefitted from their early work together. Fuzzy was finally given due recognition by being featured in films like: FUZZY SETTLES DOWN (PRC, 1944) and HIS BROTHER'S GHOST (PRC, 1945). However, my favorite Fuzzy film is GANGSTER'S DEN (PRC, 1945). This script pitted him against B-Western veterans Emmett Lynn and Charles King, and the laughs dominated the action in this low-budget PRC classic.

As a kid, I was able to see these PRC films with Fuzzy in re-release at the Gem Theater in Kingsport, Tennessee, for ten cents in the early 1950s. A traveling film show also came to an old schoolhouse in my community and frequently showed Buster Crabbe and Fuzzy films. The last and worst of the Fuzzy St. John Western features with Lash LaRue were shown at the Center Theater in my hometown. My second chance to see these films was on television, but my favorite time to see Fuzzy St. John was when I first started collecting 16mm films in the early 1970s.

At that time, his films were plentiful on the 16mm market, but the quality was poor because they had been shown so many times by people like me. Maybe this was also a favorite time because I got to introduce these films to my son, who also grew to love the physical comedy of Fuzzy.

I saw Fuzzy once in person at the Center Theater with my Dad. It was about 1951 and he appeared on the same bill with "Little" Jimmy Dickens and his band. Lash also came to my hometown twice during the early 1950s. The feature that day was THE DALTONS' WOMEN (Western Adventure, 1950). Lash and Fuzzy were only fourth and fifth in the cast, but this was a typical Lash LaRue B-Western with more women than usual and an 80 minute running time. Fuzzy brought the amazing bicycle routine to the stage that day, but I laughed at the trademark physical comedy moves of Fuzzy lots more on that occasion. For that nine-year-old kid, Fuzzy was a silent comedian performing on a stage filled with sound! Long live the legend of Fuzzy Q. Jones. He is one of the many reasons why I still love watching B-Westerns.

Billy Weathersby: Saturdays were very special for me and to absolutely everyone I knew during my childhood because that was "cowboy day" at the picture show. My friends and I spent the first half of the week talking about the previous Saturday's movie and the second half of the week talking about the upcoming Saturday's movie. We would talk about the Wild Bill Elliott movie or The Durango Kid movie, but if it was a Lash movie, we referred to it as a Lash LaRue and Fuzzy movie. I have read that Fuzzy was a superstar in Germany, and their lobby cards and movie titles showed Fuzzy with top billing. All of my friends liked Fuzzy the best of the sidekicks. I had not seen a B-Western in ages until the videotape explosion, and I re-discovered Al St. John. Even though I had not forgotten him, I found Fuzzy's humor still held up decades later. He was full of surprises, and he could be deadly serious when the occasion presented itself. He incorporated his experiences as a tumbler, acrobat, and facial expressions into his performances. To me, he was hilarious (while other sidekicks were occasionally funny) without being ridiculously silly. In LaRue's BORDER FEUD (PRC, 1947), Fuzzy is putting his and Lash's horses in the barn, and his eyes lock on Lash's whip. After looking around, Fuzzy took the whip, and tried to imitate Lash with it with hilarious and pain-filled results. When the conversation between us old-timers goes to the Westerns, we all talk about the way Fuzzy could roll a cigarette with one hand. That took skill and talent and he made it look so easy. He even had his own way of sliding off a horse and stepping down from a step, etc. He even did this in John Wayne's movie, RIDERS OF DESTINY (Monogram, 1933), in which Mr. St. John portrayed one of the baddies. I consider Fuzzy's place in the movie business as a true veteran, but to me and my friends, Fuzzy Q. Jones will always be number one because he was the best at his craft. Lash LaRue was a man of gimmicks (whip, tilted hat, black outfit, and his walk) and he really needed Fuzzy in his movies. I personally feel that Fuzzy did his best work in the Buster Crabbe movies because they seemed to complement each other so well.

Grady Franklin (former publisher of *The Western Film*): I never did care too much for Fuzzy St. John. And even less for the other Fuzzy (Knight). However, Fuzzy Q. did have a great career before he got into Westerns. I never cared for his Billy the Kid or Lash films. Mostly anything after 1940, I liked not. I did appreciate his work in Westerns of the 1930s, especially the movies of Hoppy, Tex, Tom Tyler, Jack Randall, George Houston, and some others. With guys tossed in to provide lighter moments, I never appreciated them unless they did something to help the hero. Sometimes, it would be a singer such as Ray Whitley (instead of comic relief). This attitude is because of my upbringing in the hills during the Depression. No time to be a kid. Therefore, no time for nonsense.

Colin Momber (publisher of British publication *Wrangler's Roost*): I think Fuzzy St. John was the quintessential sidekick, and was more of a real sidekick than Gabby. He was resourceful and contributed to the action, but had his silly moments. As far as I've heard, all who worked with him loved him.

Larry Hopper: Putting a finger on why I, or anyone, liked Al is difficult because he was so good at what he did. A dazed gaze, a knowing look that expressed ignorance of the subject, and his wonderful physical comedy put him steps ahead of Smiley Burnette. Fuzzy was satire of himself; Smiley was plain non-contextual Buffoonery.

Jim Hamby: as kid, I thought he was the greatest sidekick, but as I grew older and continued watching B-Westerns, I moved Gabby above Fuzzy as my favorite. I think Fuzzy was his best with Buster Crabbe and maybe working with Lash was next. You could always depend on Fuzzy for a good laugh. Fuzzy and Gabby were the two best sidekicks, and made a definite contribution to the B-Western film.

Jim Vecchio: I believe Fuzzy was a comic genius just short of Stan Laurel. He had the knack of walking down a make-believe cowboy street and planning all sorts of pratfalls and comic escapades that he would, on film, execute to perfection. I see him as a sort of comic parallel to Jock Mahoney who walked down a street, imagined his heroic stunts, and then set them into practice for the camera. We don't have many visionaries like these anymore, only egos who want big bucks and fame.

I once took some grad courses in writing for the visual media. One of them involved screenplays and was taught by Alan Sloane, who authored many notable movie and TV screenplays, including "East Side, West Side". He said George C. Scott always came in drunk, but played his role to perfection. The other was taught by a man named Abel (Rudy or Ray) who directed many vintage TV shows, including the Buster Crabbe's TV show. He said that Buster always came in drunk. I guess many stars were driven by alcohol, unfortunately.

(Note: Crabbe was arrested for DUI in Los Angeles in December 1946, and in New York in late January 1959.)

Years later, I would read that Al St. John was quite a drinker. I have since then always imagined Fuzzy and Buster, off the set, doing quite a bit of drinking together, having their laughs, which somehow translated into an on-screen camaraderie. (This is not to condone drinking, but I always wondered if that was part of the "cement" that held that "team" together.)

Of course, as Christians, we know that so many people need Christ, but they replace Him with things that eventually do them harm, like alcohol. I used to be the "co-sheikh" of a "Sons of the Desert" tent, but quit when I realized this was causing myself and others to abuse alcohol. But

I remember that many of the laughs and guffaws we enjoyed were fueled from over-drinking. At the National Convention in Los Angeles - that was all many people did. Some stars, like Ken Maynard, eventually met their downfall because of this. I do not know enough about Al St. John to make this statement, but I have wondered if drinking helped him discover his character and then eventually lead to the diminishing of his screen presence. At the very least, he was the tail-end of a dying breed of comic geniuses who perfected their stunts before a silent camera, and parlayed their experience into a second vocation on the sound screen. I do know that overseas (in the mode of Jerry Lewis) Al's star shown brighter than in the United States.

Other parallels to Stan Laurel would be the fact that just one look at Fuzzy would establish his character in your mind, but you always looked forward to see what he would be saying or doing next. I never felt that way about Buster Crabbe, or any of the other cowboys he "side-kicked". Once Fuzzy was established in the movie, he became my central focus. His character had enough of a versatility to afford us surprise, as in some scenes he was an awkward and stumbling nincompoop and, in others, he would save the day and without his presence, the hero might have met fatal results. I did feel that in some scenes he took unnecessary jabbing and teasing, but he always went with the flow. In the end, it wasn't Gabby, but Fuzzy who had a movie title and movie premise driven by his character (FUZZY SETTLES DOWN, HIS BROTHER'S GHOST). I always wondered what CAPTAIN GALLANT would have been like, had it been St. John, not KNIGHT, who portrayed the "Fuzzy" character. I think it would have been an entirely more memorable program if infused with his creative energy.

My favorite line of Fuzzy's was when he once responded to a remark by saying, "Tell that to someone who ain't got no sense. I use that a lot with my wife!"

Gene Blottner (promoter of the Williamsburg Film Festival): Al "Fuzzy" St. John was one of my favorite sidekicks. He enlivened many Westerns, especially those of PRC. His physical comedy delighted both adult and juvenile audiences. Fuzzy worked well with various Western stars. He had great chemistry with both Buster Crabbe and Lash LaRue that was apparent to moviegoers.

Clyde Lester: My thought in general is that Fuzzy is the most overlooked of all the B sidekicks. I would put Fuzzy behind Smiley in the number two place, just ahead of Gabby. Fuzzy made his slapstick look very natural compared to some others. He worked best with Buster Crabbe closely followed by Lash. He really helped these two and they sure needed it. If he made Buster look good, he was one heck of an actor. I would advise anyone to look at his movies with Buster and Lash and just study him and forget the rest. You will truly appreciate him.

Bruce Hickey (fan from New Zealand): After Gabby Hayes and Raymond Hatton, daylight is next. But if I had to choose one from all the rest of the sidekicks, it'd be Fuzzy. I haven't seen him with George Houston or Fred Scott, but he worked well with Bob Steele, Buster Crabbe, and Lash LaRue. He was definitely an asset to the PRC films.

Buddy Bryant: I thought Fuzzy was good, but not nearly as good as Gabby. A good acrobat, I guess. Years ago, my grand uncle (Wallace Osborne) traveled with the Tommy Scott Ozark Music Show, and Fuzzy was with them. Uncle Wallace said that Fuzzy would just sit in his hotel room and drink whiskey until time to appear on stage. He would then walk across the street to the theater and do his part and go right back to his room to drink. Many may not want to hear this kind of stuff, but that's the way it was. It seems like Fuzzy never got any further than the lower end of the B-Westerns. During his time on stage, he would let some kid come up and pull his beard just to prove it was real. I only saw his act once. I think he was about as good with one cowboy star as the other. I guess I was not overly impressed with him, but maybe if he had done more at Republic, I would have appreciated him more.

Ronnie Glass: I always thought that he was a little too silly for a sidekick. But to think that he was born in 1893, and some of his movies were made in the 1940s and early 1950s, that is not a young man performing some of the most amazing acrobatic stunts and tricks. I always think of the way he crossed his legs in a chair, or mounted a horse and the great bicycle tricks. What agility he had!

Joe Copeland: I liked him a lot, especially his comedic, physical actions like getting on or off a horse, bicycle riding, the way he had of stepping down off a raised sidewalk, and standing on his head up against a wall after getting hit by a bad guy. I rate him a distant 2nd behind Gabby Hayes. I thought he was best with Buster Crabbe. Without him, the Crabbe movies would be very lacking.

Ross Pitt: I always thought of him as a character actor, not as a comic. To me, he was not "funny" funny, but his versatility acquired during his Keystone Cop days with Sennett was outstanding. I don't know of a sidekick that had the facial expressions and could do the body movements that Fuzzy could do. He was very funny in that respect.

Also, I always thought him to be a good Western actor. He made Westerns with almost all your top B-Western actors like, of course, Buster Crabbe, Hopalong Cassidy, Fred Scott, Richard Arlen, Robert Livingston, Don "Red" Barry, just to name a few. He was a henchman, a drunk, a teller, a deputy, a bum, you name it, and he could play the part. I really don't think we looked at his acting ability and in this respect, to me, he was underrated as an actor. If you will notice in a lot of Westerns made in the 1930s and 1940s by production companies like Spectrum, Mascot, Monogram, PRC, and Grand National, you are likely to see Fuzzy in various character roles. He really came to the front as a "sidekick" with Fred Scott and then Buster Crabbe. I consider those his hey-days.

R. T. Blackwood (fan from England) Writing purely as a fan, to my mind Fuzzy may have been a wee man, but he was a big asset to PRC. Of the Western sidekicks, I would place Fuzzy at No. 3, after George Hayes at No. 1 and Andy Clyde at No. 2. If, however, he had been grabbed by Republic and partnered with one of their stars, with the exception of "Rocky" Lane to whom humor was an alien concept, then with better scripts, production values, and directors, he may well have overtaken Andy Clyde.

It could be argued that, on occasion, his slapstick could become irritating and, as an adult, I would probably agree, but, as a child, I probably lapped it up. Offsetting that, at least the dialogue given to him was neither childish nor silly and was generally confined to helping along the plot and PRC, to their credit, often gave him his own scenes and the chance to show that, if required, he could handle the serious stuff, HIS BROTHER'S GHOST (PRC, 1945) being a good example. I have not had the chance to watch any of the Fred Scott films, but from looking at stills from the films, it would seem that Fuzzy was refining his Western garb, and therefore, probably his characterization. Here is how I view Fuzzy with some other cowboy heroes:

George Houston: By this time, he had his character in full flow, and worked well enough with Houston even joining in the odd song, but, as we well know, George Houston, while not the worst actor to strap on a six gun, never seem completely relaxed on the Lone Rider films, being more suited to the operatic stage.

Robert Livingston only worked with Fuzzy in a few films and had no chance of establishing a decent rapport and, in any case, I always thought that Livingston wanted to be the star.

Bob Steele's Billy the Kid films tacked on a third hero, normally Carleton Young, which gave Fuzzy a little less screen time. Bob Steele was always a bundle of pent-up energy, and the scripts never really allowed him to have any relaxed banter with St. John.

Without a doubt, Buster Crabbe was the best of Fuzzy's partners. They worked well off each other and everything just seemed to gel. In their hard-riding sequences, they rode side by side. Very rarely did Falcon outstrip Fuzzy's rather plain mount and, on the odd occasion, Fuzzy's horse could be seen edging ahead, and there were some heroes we could name who would never stand for that! The only thing that didn't work was when the film had to end on a piece of Fuzzy's slapstick. Buster's laughter was the most unconvincing bit of acting seen on the screen.

By the time Fuzzy joined Lash LaRue, he could sleepwalk through his routines, and may well have done that. Now, Fuzzy's films were hitting the bottom of a very deep barrel. And Lash was a totally different personality to Buster, conveying a "tough guy" image to Buster's easy-going style, but Fuzzy took the change in his comical stride. And, as poor as the films were with Lash, he would come in at No. 2 of Fuzzy's best partners.

So in order, Buster Crabbe, Lash LaRue, George Houston, Bob Steele, Robert Livingston, and Fred Scott (I may be unfair to Mr. Scott): My favorite Fuzzy moment, no doubt shared by many, was Fuzzy's arrival on horseback where he would swing his right leg over the horse's neck and, in slow motion, slide down from the saddle. As a bonus, he would hitch up his trousers when expecting trouble. Hats off to Al "Fuzzy" St. John, one of the "Best of the West."

Jerry Baumann: Honestly, I didn't care for him at all. He probably was most tolerable with Lash and Buster Crabbe, but usually his roles were always more silly rather than believable. Unlike Gabby Hayes and Andy Clyde who were capable of tracking down outlaws and still add humor.

Paul Dellinger (Dellinger has written many articles on Westerns and serials): I can remember the first time I saw Al St. John or, as I always think of him, Fuzzy Q. Jones. I was in the first grade, and two of my cousins had introduced me to the weekend double feature at our hometown's "old" theater. I was sitting with them in the front row, watching STAGECOACH OUTLAWS (PRC, 1945) with Buster Crabbe and Fuzzy.

But I was relatively unsophisticated in the ways of B-Westerns. When Johnny Mack Brown and Raymond Hatton rode off on separate trails at the end of one of their movies, I found it sad because I thought they were separating forever. When Tex Ritter and Dave O'Brien came to blows in THREE IN THE SADDLE (PRC, 1945), I turned to my cousins and said plaintively, "But I thought they were friends." ("They are," I was assured.) And when Fuzzy seemed to be one of the bad guys and told Buster, aka Billy Carson, to stay away from him, I didn't understand that Fuzzy was impersonating an outlaw so he and Billy could bring the baddies to justice.

I soon figured it out, when Billy was snooping in the lobby of a dilapidated hotel where the outlaws were hatching their plots and was almost caught by one of them. The rest of the gang, on an upper floor, rushes to catch the snooper – until Fuzzy "falls" in front of them, and they all go tumbling down the stairs.

That was my introduction to Buster and Fuzzy. I had no idea that Al St. John had been working in movies since in the early silent movie days. Only later did I see some of his earlier Westerns, courtesy of film collector/scholar Mack Houston: THE OKLAHOMA CYCLONE, a Tiffany 1930 movie in which Bob Steele "sings" (making him a singing cowboy even before Gene Autry) and is befriended by an outlaw named Slim (St. John) in the gang he infiltrates. In fact, the beardless St. John ends up sacrificing his life for his "pal" in a touching scene which proved he could act, given the chance. Three years later, there was RIDERS OF DESTINY (Monogram, 1933) in which John Wayne "sang" and St. John played one of the outlaws. Early on, he and another villain are roped by Duke, aka "Singin' Sandy." "Get together!" Sandy orders, and the two embrace each other as best they can while lassoed. St. John takes his free hand and moves his other hand into the correct position, an early bit of what looked like improvisation and a hint of his comedy capers to come.

I can remember my second Fuzzy movie even more vividly: HIS BROTHER'S GHOST (PRC, 1945), another Billy Carson opus. In this one, St. John has a dual role – as Andy Jones, a leader of ranchers against an outlaw band who seems to be a friend of Billy's, and later as Jonathan, or Fuzzy, Andy's twin brother.

Early in the picture, there's a raid on Andy's ranch and, in the ensuing gun battle, Andy is shot. Even there, St. John does his fall with comedic flair. But he gives another touching performance, as he passes the torch to his twin brother, who impersonates Andy and makes the outlaws believe they are being haunted by Andy's ghost.

Only later would I learn that St. John began his sidekick role at PRC with his former co-star Bob Steele, who filmed a half-dozen pictures there as a cleaned-up version of Billy the Kid. The only time I had seen a Bob Steele movie was the 1945 Cinecolor horse story WILDFIRE (Screen Guild), but my father, who took me, assured me that Steele was an extraordinary cowboy. His Billy series had only run from 1940 to 1941, before my movie-going time. (I did catch up a little bit when some showed up on TV.)

Then Buster Crabbe took over the role, continuing with Fuzzy as the comic sidekick, in a whopping 36 pictures between 1941 and 1946. The character had shifted from Billy the Kid to Billy Carson three years before I saw any of them, and I only got there for the last two years of the Billy Carsons (which still amounted to more than a dozen pictures).

I had missed Fuzzy's first movies with Fred Scott, and the ones where he continued playing the same character in other oaters with Jack Randall, George Houston, Lee Powell, and Art Jarrett, and even as a sidekick in his pre-Fuzzy days alongside such stalwarts as Tex Ritter, Tom Tyler, and Guinn "Big Boy" Williams in a 1935 early version of William Colt MacDonald's "Three Mesquiteers," reduced to two. (Fuzzy was in the role which would later be assumed by the likes of Bob Livingston, John Wayne, and Tom Tyler.)

After Buster Crabbe departed, I would not see Fuzzy again until PRC began its Lash LaRue series, 20 features between 1947 and 1952 with the studio name changing to Eagle-Lion and then Western Adventure Productions/Screen Guild. The only change for Fuzzy was that, in the later productions, his status seemed to be upgraded because his sidearm changed from a black handle to a white one and his horse from plain brown to pinto (much like Raymond Hatton in the Johnny Mack series at Monogram).

I had seen LaRue in only one of the three Eddie Dean Cinecolor Westerns where he provided support, WILD WEST (PRC, 1946). It hit our town's main theater while Eddie's and Lash's B's were getting underway at the weekend theater. It was good to see Fuzzy back on the screen when the LaRues started turning up.

My sidekick preferences were those who appeared competent, like Hatton, or "Gabby" Hayes (usually), or Chito (usually) to the bumblers like Smiley and Cannonball. Fuzzy fell somewhere between the extremes, but was competent enough for me. He could fail to stifle a sneeze and give away his and Lash's position to the outlaws, but he could also bring a posse to save the day in record time. In KING OF THE BULLWHIP (Western Adventure, 1951), he all but mows down the entire outlaw gang – with a slingshot! There is also a great scene where Lash is in a saloon fistfight and one of his opponent's friends starts to ease a pistol out of a holster to make the odds uneven. Fuzzy, standing next to the friend at the bar, eases his own pistol out first. When the baddie glances over, Fuzzy just shakes his head "no."

His physical comedy was always surprising, too. Gabby may have been the better actor, but Fuzzy could keep audiences amused by seemingly improvising pratfalls and other routines that had nothing to do with the story but were still fun. In later years when I saw some of his Buster Crabbe movies, I realized the story was often more about Fuzzy than about Billy Carson.

There were a lot of Fuzzy clones out there. A comic-book Westerner named Wild Bill Pecos had a Fuzzy-like sidekick named Nuggets Nugent. On radio's "Straight Arrow," the Comanche warrior who pretended by day to be rancher Steve Adams had a sidekick named Packy McCloud, voiced by Fred Howard, and, when we heard him, we knew he looked like Fuzzy – and, when the comic book version of the show hit the stands, we found out we were right.

But the original never got his own comic book, although Gabby and Smiley Burnette did at Fawcett, the same company which gave us the Lash LaRue comics. The series occasionally incorporated Lash's twin brother, The Frontier Phantom, from the movies (mainly OUTLAW COUNTRY (Western Adventure/Screen Guild, 1949), but also THE FRONTIER PHANTOM (Western Adventure, 1952), the final picture in the series, which was largely a re-telling of OUTLAW COUNTRY). But no Fuzzy.

That would change on three occasions. Fawcett also published the comic-book versions of Rocky Lane and Monte Hale, and adapted several of their movies into comic-book form in either Motion Picture Comics or Fawcett Movie Comics. Lash got the same treatment on three occasions – adaptations of THE VANISHING OUTPOST, THE THUNDERING TRAIL (Western Adventure, 1951) and KING OF THE BULLWHIP (Western Adventure, 1951). And, in those comics, we also at long last got Fuzzy.

Occasionally, some of the B-Western veterans would visit local theaters for personal appearances. That was how I got my first looks at Dub "Cannonball" Taylor, Lash LaRue, Tim Holt, and even Tarzan's Cheetah. But the first of the Western stars to appear in my hometown was none other than Fuzzy.

Talk about a treat! It was the first time I had ever seen one of my screen idols in person. At this stage, the main thing I remember was that the announcement of Fuzzy's appearance mentioned that someone from the audience would be chosen to tug on his beard to see if it was real. The picture on the screen showed someone really struggling to pull Fuzzy's beard off, and Fuzzy struggling right back. However, when a youngster was brought to the stage to do the pulling, no sooner did the boy lay hands on Fuzzy's beard when Fuzzy fired a blank from his holstered pistol, and the boy hastily let go.

Fuzzy must have had a longer movie career than any of the cowboy sidekicks. He certainly entertained me. I still miss him.

(Note: Tommy Scott related another story about Fuzzy's beard getting pulled: "Fuzzy loved to read and would spend hours reading Westerns. He was sitting back stage one day, and some guy, who thought he was smart, walked past Fuzzy and reached over and pulled Fuzzy's long beard and said, 'Is that real? He went past Fuzzy three times, and each time he repeated the same remark. When he walked by the fourth time and reached for Fuzzy's beard, the words formed on his lips, but he never got to say them. Fuzzy kicked him right in the crotch and said in a quiet voice, 'Is that real?' and went back to his reading. The man had a fit and said in a strained voice, 'I'll see that you don't work here anymore. Fuzzy just kept on reading.")

FUZZY ON TOUR

(Although I have already addressed some about of Fuzzy's touring, I received addition information from John Brooker and Jimmy Glover which is added here. Brooker had telephone conversations with musician Barney Miller, and showman Tommy Scott. Glover provided a photo of Fuzzy on one of his tours.)

The writing was on the wall for the B-Westerns in the late 1940s, and in 1948 Fuzzy teamed up with a young country music group, The Blue Sky Cowboys, to go out on tour. The steel guitarist with the group was Barney Miller who recalled his days on the road with Fuzzy.

Barney Miller: "I started playing steel guitar when I was 13 and in a couple of years I was on the road for my first tour. It was with Dub Taylor, who was known as 'Cannonball' to movie fans. Dub played the xylophone, and I got extra money for dismantling it and setting it up again at the next show.

"One of the reasons we got to work with Dub was because Joe Haugh, owner of the Joy Theater chain, promoted many live shows. Haugh and his wife lived in Meridian, Mississippi, and he thought our band was the best around at the time. The Joy Theater chain was the largest in the Southeast, and we played them all. We also worked with Bobby 'Little Beaver' Blake, Robert Livingston and Bob Steele in the Meridian area.

"When we finished the tour with Dub, he went back to California and recommended us to Fuzzy who was to make his first tour with his own show.

"Our group worked in theaters with him for 2-3 years. The band consisted of Sonny, Slim, Peewee Burns, and me playing steel guitar, bass fiddle and flat guitar. We would play 20-30 minutes and then Fuzzy would be introduced for his act. We stayed on stage to assist him in several of his routines.

"In one of the routines, he would ask an 8-10 year-old to come up onto the stage to pull his beard to let the kids see if it was real or not. While the kid was pulling on Fuzzy's beard, Fuzzy would slip his gun out of the holster and fire the gun behind him. This would cause the kid to go berserk, along with the audience.

"Everything he did was to perfection, on stage and off. After arriving at a theater we would go over everything, especially the sound. Fuzz wanted to make sure everyone could see and hear the dialog, music, etc.

"The size of the stage was always a problem: sometimes it was very small which resulted in his changing his routine. This also meant changes for us because we assisted him all through his act. A good size stage meant more acrobatics.

"When Fuzzy would say 'Show time!' We had to have everything ready for our first tune. Sometimes I would do an instrumental while the other band members were doing a sound check, only no one knew it was really a sound check except us. We played and sung Western songs, plus the songs that were popular on radio at that time.

"One of Fuzzy's bits of business was to roll a cigarette with one hand. He'd be in the center of the stage and pull out his sack of Bull Durham smoking tobacco He'd get just one cigarette paper from the pack, which he could made hilarious. Next he poured the tobacco into the paper, twisting his hand around, rolling the cigarette all in one motion, and putting it in his lips. It was very funny. He just kept the audience laughing. Then he'd take a match out of his pants pocket, drop it on the floor, look for it, and pretend to trip over it. He'd pick up the match and turn a cartwheel back to the center of the stage where he struck the match on the back of his pant leg, light the cigarette and smoke it (this was to let the audience know it was a real cigarette). Then he'd stomp out the match on the stage floor, pretend burn his foot, and hop around on one foot. All this would sometimes take 2-3 minutes.

"Fuzzy was the only one in the world who could pull that stunt off. His part on stage was about 20 minutes … on a smaller stage it was about 15 minutes or so. He was a master of perfection in all his routines.

"Towards the end of his act he would get more serious and tell about his movie career, his ranch, family, etc. He would always give credit to each one of the performers.

"In show business it was then, and is now, very difficult to master an audience from start to finish but Fuzz could do it better than anyone I have ever known. He could hold the audience in the palm of his hand.

"Our part could change, but mostly we would play about 20 minutes more after Fuzzy's performance. Then he would come back and do a little more, but our band stayed on the stage for the entire show. That part was hard and it took practice for perfection.

"On stage Fuzzy demanded 100 per cent from everyone. We had to do everything just right ... it was his way or the highway. Our shows always seemed to go over well.

"We worked one night stands at theaters from New York to Florida, seven days a week and three shows a day, and he never missed a line or a show, ever!!!

"Fuzzy kept his family with him on the road. His second wife June was the boss and looked after the finances. Fuzzy had lost a fortune in the Great Depression years.

"Raymond, his step-son with June, was the show manager. Since I was the youngest, June looked after me a little more than the others. We were not allowed to smoke or say bad words, and our wardrobe – all western dress – was always clean and pressed. Fuzzy wore the same outfit on stage as he did in the movies. He also did all the stunts himself.

"His favorite movie person was Fatty Arbuckle from the Keystone Cops era – he talked about Fatty being his uncle. Fuzzy appeared in several silent comedy films with Fatty, and with others.

"The cowboy star he liked working with most was Buster Crabbe but the most popular one with the fans was Lash LaRue. I didn't get along well with Lash. He was self-centered and quick to lose his temper. I'm glad I never worked much with him.

"I helped Fuzzy with one of his hobbies, which was collecting police badges. In every town he would invite local police officers to the show and they would give him a badge. By the end of our tour, he had several badges.

"He loved show business. He really enjoyed the tours. Fuzzy treated his fans extra nice, signing pictures, etc. We did a lot of extra shows. I know he had more friends than the average star back then.

"Fuzzy was a good Catholic. One day he asked me to learn to play 'Ava Maria.' I had never heard or seen the music to that song, so I asked him if he could help me find the song and I would try and play it. A week or two later, a Hawaiian group was playing near us. He asked them to come by and play 'Ava Maria' for me. Well they played the song beautifully, and I noticed Fuzz had tears in his eyes while they were playing. So I learned the song, not as well as the Hawaiian group, but I would often play it backstage for him.

"We all did very well financially. He paid us every week and there was always some extra money for me to send home. I'm not sure if he earned more from the movies or the tours. Our band was very good, but I thought we were paid more than we were worth! Fuzz always said nice things to help us improve.

"We traveled in two cars on the tour. Fuzz had a long station wagon, and he and June sat in front. He was always the driver. I would ride in the middle seat. Fuzzy's wife was a very smart lady, and was in command of everything. Their son Raymond had his own car and was mostly two or three days ahead of us with the publicity. Fuzz really loved his family.

"Raymond married a girl from Mississippi and went back to California when the tour ended. June passed away some time after that. She had a special seat for traveling in the car. Her health had deteriorated as the tour went on.

"By the time of our second tour with Fuzzy, around the early 1950s, he was with his new wife Flo Belle. She was an English lady who played cowbells on the show, but I didn't think her act fit in with what we were doing. In my eyes, she was not a replacement for June.

"We had the same band and played the same show, only this time we were in the middle states, but Fuzz was a changed man. To be truthful, he drank way too much. But it never affected the show. He was still a trouper in every sense of the word. Shortly after that, I left the show and went into the Army. After my discharge, I went into TV. I did five shows weekly and worked weekends with Opry groups at concerts.

"I married my Mary and moved back to Mobile, Alabama. One day I was looking at the paper when I saw the Tommy Scott Show was in town and Fuzzy St. John was the star. I got Mary and I raced down to see him. We arrived long before show time. Fuzzy and I had a really great time, going over the good old days.

"When the show started he had difficulty walking on stage. I could tell he was very sick, but he managed it and did a very fine show. Afterwards, I escorted him back to his dressing room and said, 'Fuzz let me take you home with me. You can't do this anymore. You don't owe these people anything. I'll get you in the hospital. I'll take care of you.' He looked at me and said 'It's too late, but it's so good to see you again.' I knew that would be the last time I'd see him. Three days later, on January 21 1963, he died in Lyons, Georgia.

"Fuzz was an inspiration to me. He is greatly responsible for my success in music, and set me on a good path to walk all through my life."

(Tommy Scott, the last of the traditional medicine showmen, first hit the road over 75 years ago, and since then has played in more than 29,000 different towns across the United States and Canada. His shows covered just about every aspect of entertainment, including comedy, country music and circus acts. He often worked with B-Western personalities, including Tim McCoy, Johnny Mack Brown and Sunset Carson. It was in 1956 that Fuzzy St. John joined his show.)

Tommy Scott: "Fuzzy had operated his own show for several years but when he joined me he was playing mostly weekends – doing his act and introducing one of his Western movies. He was pretty much down and out, He once had money but he'd lost it.

"He worked for me seven years – 350 days a year – in a different town every day. We'd pack up just after Thanksgiving and start again the first of January.

"He had a reputation as a drinker on his Western pictures. But when he came to me I told him I didn't allow drinking on my shows, and if he needed to have a drink after the show he had to be sure he was ready to travel the first thing the next morning.

"He was as good as gold with me. As far as I know he did very little drinking during his time with me. Some of his colleagues from his movie days would not believe he wasn't drinking heavily.

"Fuzzy was a very funny man on stage - he had a 20 minute spot. He was very athletic. He could do a backwards somersault on the spot and land back on his feet.

"He was one of the nicest men you could ever wish to meet. He loved reading. You could always find him in a corner reading a book. He was very shy offstage – he didn't like to talk to people about his life and his movies. And yet he would go along to Lion's Club meetings and give them a talk for free.

"His wife Flo also worked for me. She was a great self-promoter. Her act was playing cowbells. She was more interested in herself than Fuzzy.

"Wherever we went he left the stage, the audience was laughing. The night before he died he had to be carried on stage but he went on and gave one of his best performances. I think he knew it would be his last show and he wanted to go out in style. He certainly did that."

Calvin Ruff, an accordionist with Lash LaRue and Fuzzy on personal appearances, related the following story to western film fan Jimmy Glover:

"Calvin was assigned by Fuzzy's wife to watch over him while they were on the road. As you know, Fuzzy was scamper to the nearest liquor store. Calvin told me that one day, toward the end when Fuzzy was thinking about retiring, Fuzzy offered to sell him his gun and holster set and uniform for $50. Calvin told him to not sell it to anyone because it should remain in his family, and turned down the offer. He later discovered that Fuzzy sold it to someone else about a week later."

Fuzzy doesn't look very happy in this early 1950s photo.

Calvin Ruff, Lash LaRue, and Fuzzy.

(Shortly before her death Fuzzy's wife Flo wrote the letter the letter below to John Brooker. It was dated February 12, 1972, and sent from the Double F Ranch (Fuzzy & Flo), Homosassa Springs, Florida. She said she was 'approaching 72 and very well and healthy.)

Flo Belle St. John: "I was born in England, and in 1960-61 Al and I were at U.S. air bases in England, performing three miles from where I attended school in Letchworth in 1906.

"Al was my beloved pard and entertainer of countless friends and admirers. He lived to make people happy and would do anything to assist the less fortunate. I was his manager in his later years. I am trying to keep Al's memory alive by raising money for retarded and handicapped children charities, schools and the aged.

"Fred Scott, an early star in Al's sky, has said he would help me and Tex Ritter has promised to do a charity appearance along with a showing of SING COWBOY SING, which Al was his sidekick.

Flo St. John

"George Houston was his favorite singing star. On the day George died he phoned to say he would be calling for a visit the next morning. His death was a great shock to Al who had a similar farewell – very fast and painless, thank God!

"Another favorite of Al's was John Cason who was left-handed and had a reputation for being one of the fastest guns in Hollywood. In the winter months Al would spend evenings with the folks he loved and worked with, going over stories and incidents time and time again.

"I say with regret that I never mention Lash LaRue for had I not rescued Al from that studio he would never have lived as long as he did. They worked him to death in those films, getting him to do slapstick and heavy falls although he was almost 60. I wanted him out of those movies because I thought they'd end up killing him."

(Note: We apology for the poor condition of Mrs. St. John's picture. it is the only known photo of her available to Western film fans.)

TRAIL'S END

Fuzzy was working for the Tommy Scott Medicine Show when he died. According to Scott, Fuzzy never missed a performance during his nearly five years with the show. Scott said that on their last show in Florida, Fuzzy had complained about not feeling well, and when Scott told him to take the night off, Fuzzy refused saying, "as long as you pay me, I'm going out there and do my work," which he did. Scott said it was the best performance he'd seen Fuzzy do.

Scott told of Fuzzy's death: "They arrived at the motel where Flo Belle (Fuzzy's wife) had made reservations for them to stay. There was a small fruit stand nearby and Fuzzy, who loved grapes, asked Flo if she would go buy some for him. She told him to go into the motel and get settled, and then she would buy the grapes. She was probably gone for less than 10 minutes. When she went back to the motel, she found Fuzzy lying across the bed, dead of a heart attack. He was not an old man by our standards of today; he was simply worn out. Fuzzy's age was given as 70, but I feel he was actually 72. According to Fuzzy's wishes, he was cremated, and we had a memorial service for him in Georgia. His ashes were sent back to California, and his wardrobe was sent to a Western museum."

You might say Fuzzy's last appearance came in 2001 in the Tommy Scott production which aired over PBS entitled *Still Ramblin'*, a documentary that follows the career of Scott. Fuzzy appears in archive footage with other stars and performers who traveled with the medicine show.

It is difficult to determine the number of Fuzzy's screen appearances. The American Film Institute (AFI) lists his appearances in 139 features. The International Movie Database lists 244 films, including shorts, but even Fuzzy himself had no ideas of his number of movies.

Fuzzy gets the drop on "Doc" Tommy Scott and his pal. Luke.

FUZZY'S OBITUARY

(Note: The obit differs somewhat from Scott's story.)

Al St. John, 'Fuzzy Jones,' Dies in Lyons
Lyons, Ga., Jan. 22

A character well known to Western fans – Fuzzy Q. Jones – is dead at the age of 70. Fuzzy, who in real life was Al St. John, collapsed Monday at Lyons in the arms of his wife. St. John and his wife Flo Belle Moore were scheduled to make a personal appearance Monday at nearby Vidalia.

So ends the story of Al St. John – our beloved Fuzzy Q. Jones. As youngsters, he made us laugh, and we still manage a smile when we think of him today.

FUZZY IN THE HEADLINES

(From *The Los Angeles Times*)

May 14, 1916: **FATTY ARBUCKLE TO APPEAR IN KEYSTONE COP COMEDY**: Supporting Arbuckle with be Irene Wallace, Al St. John, and Minta Dupree in the great laugh provoker, THE OTHER MAN.

December 9, 1917: **COMEDIAN INJURED WHILE FILMING**: While filming scenes on the desert near Yermo, California with Fatty Arbuckle, Al St. John was injured, and the filming is expected to be delayed. It is unknown the extent of the little comedian's injuries.

(Note: Yermo is a town in San Bernardino County, California. It is located 13 miles east of Barstow on Interstate 15, just south of the Calico Mountains.)

July 29, 1919: **AL ST. JOHN SIGNS WITH PARAMOUNT**: Comedian happy with contract and ready for work.

December 3, 1919, "Kid" McCoy, an ex-pugilist, and Al St. John, a motion picture actor, today entered into an agreement by which McCoy will train Babe Ruth for 30 days, and if his report is favorable, it is said St. John will finance campaign of the outfielder to obtain a match with Jack Dempsey, heavyweight champion.

"I have always wanted to be a professional boxer," said Ruth tonight, "but I gave up any future I might have had in that game to play baseball. If McCoy and St John think I have any future I am willing to do everything they ask."

(Note: Of course, with Ruth being a premier baseball star, this did not materialize.)

May 10, 1920: **COMEDIAN'S FIRST STARRING ROLE**: You'll enjoy Al St. John in his first starring role, SPEED. It's riotous reels of laughter.

December 21, 1922: **COMEDIAN TO HELP AT BENEFIT SHOW**: AL St. John will perform at the Los Angeles Women's Association benefit tomorrow.

August 1, 1923: **WIFE'S PRESCRIPTION FILLED**: Mrs. Al St. John, wife of the film comedian, today had her physician's prescription filled in Judge Ralph Clock's court. Her physician advised her to divorce comedian Al St. John to save her health.

August 2, 1923: **FILM MARRIAGE GOES ON THE ROCKS**: Mrs. Al St. John was awarded interlocutory decree; gets alimony; automobile and pay for chauffeur; court allows $150 monthly for daughter.

August 6, 1923: **MIX AND ST. JOHN FEATURED**: Tom Mix is "Stepping Fast" this week at the Symphony (theater) and with him – that is, on the same bill, is Al St. John in TOPICAL ROMEO. A combination worthy of a packed house.

August 22, 1924: **CHAUFFEUR SACRIFICED**: Ex-wife of Al St. John yields point in plea for more alimony. She agrees to give up her chauffeur in exchange for more money.

September 5, 1925: **LESSON IN ETIQUETTE:** While some others offered strong objections before a traffic court judge, Al St. John, in a soft voice, says it's all his fault. Other similar traffic offenses draw jail time while St. John is only fined.

July 1, 1926: **AL ST. JOHN, MOVIE COMEDIAN, TO WED**: Al St. John, film comedian, to wed tomorrow to Miss June Price Pearce, not an actress. It is the bride's first wedding and St. John's second. The comedian was divorced by his first wife, Lillian St. John, two years ago. After a three weeks' honeymoon, the couple will settle in Hollywood.

(Note: The article is mistaken about it being June Price Pearce's first marriage because on December 24, 1924, she won a judgment against her ex-husband because he had sent her word he would "break her back" if she took him to court asking for more money.)

June 20, 1927: **ST. JOHN SAYS HE JUST "SLIPPED UP" – PLANNED TRIP TO EUROPE**: Al St. John, comedian, today faced a charge of failure to support his five- year-old daughter, who has been in the custody of Mrs. Lillian St. John since she obtained a divorce in 1923 on charges of cruelty. She was awarded $150 a month alimony. St. John surrendered to the sheriff's office yesterday when he was informed that a warrant for his arrest had been issued by a San Diego court. St. John remarried to June Price Pearce in July 1926. The warrant was issued by the San Diego authorities when it became known that the film comedian contemplated a trip to Europe with Roscoe Arbuckle, film comedian. "I slipped up on the alimony," St. John said. "I intended to pay it as soon as I could get the money." Bail was fixed at $500, which he furnished and then was released.

August 29, 1929: **ST. JOHN JAILED**: Al St. John, screen comedian, was ordered to the county jail by Superior Judge Charles Burnell for failure to maintain alimony payments.

August 30, 1929: **FILM JESTER ON ROAD GANG**: Al St. John, unemployed and faced with the obligation of supporting "three families," was sentenced to work on a road gang by Judge Charles Burnell for failing to pay alimony.

August 31, 1929: **COMEDIAN AT LIBERTY ON BAIL**: Comedian freed from road-gang sentence; bail granted pending final disposition of case; other alimony matters up on appeal. Superior Judge Burnell's treatment Thursday of alimony seekers and alimony delinquents had its echo in the District Court of Appeals here late yesterday when two of the litigants, not liking the court's particular methods of dealing with their own cases, sought a new trial before a different judge.

September 4, 1929: **THREATS SENT TO JUDGE**: Letters condemning Judge Burnell, one of them carrying a threat and signed "The Vigilantes" for committing Al St. John, motion-picture comedian, to the county road gang for his failure to keep up alimony payments, and another denouncing the Judge for refusing to allow St. John to return to work in order to make the payments.

September 29, 1929: **COURT SUSPENDS FILM COMEDIAN'S JAIL SENTENCE**: Superior Judge Rosenkranz yesterday suspended the jail sentence imposed on Al St. John, film comedian.

July 26, 1934: **BARTHELMESS BACKS CLEAN FILM DRIVE**: A couple of old time motion picture stars, Richard Barthelmess and Al St. John, dropped into town today and agreed that a little cleaning up wouldn't do the industry any harm.

June 30, 1935: **GAME ENDS UP IN A RIOT – UMPIRE GETS "SHOT"**: The screen's leading men battled to a 4-4 tie with the film comics in a baseball game here Saturday. The scorekeeper gave up trying to keep a box score because everybody tried to play every position. Bill Bakewell, pinch hitting for George Raft, used a limousine to round the bases after a hard line-drive. He wore a dress suit and a top hat. Al St. John, after a single, rode a bicycle to first base. The leading men ended the contest in the fourth inning when Jack LaRue, objecting to a decision, produced a pistol and "shot" the umpire. The real winner was a charity fund.

July 16, 1936: **AL ST. JOHN GOES OUT OF COURT INTO FILM COMEBACK**: Al St. John, comedy star of the silent films, resumed his "comeback" work today, free of a charge he failed to provide for his 17-year-old daughter. Brought into justice court here on a complaint by his former wife, Mrs. M. L. St. John, the veteran film maker testified he had "done everything in my power" towards supporting their daughter. Mrs. St. John expressed belief her former husband's attitude was "all right now," and Justice Dean Sherry found him innocent. After the session, St. John climbed into an old motor car and headed for Hollywood.

August 6, 1936: **NEW ROLE FOR ST. JOHN:** Al St. John, former comedy star, has been given a part In GAMBLING SHIP which also features Cary Grant. *(Note: St. John was not in the movie.)*

February 14, 1937: **ST. JOHN RETURNS TO THE MOVIES**: Al St. John, of the one-reel comedy days, returned to the movies for a character role In THE OUTCASTS OF POKER FLATS.

Budd Buster, Fuzzy, Mady Lawrence, Stan Jolley, Buster and John Cason.

"There they go, Fuzz."

ESSENTIAL FUZZY

I do not recall Fuzzy ever turning in a bad performance as a sidekick. The following films are the ones which I thought he was particularly impressive. I realize comedy is a personal thing, and you may have other favorites.

MOONLIGHT ON THE RANGE (Spectrum, 1937): When Killer Dane (also Fred Scott) kills Jeff's friend, Jeff (also Fred Scott) goes after him. Jeff and Dane are look-alike half brothers, and this leads Dane to make a raid dressed like Jeff. This gets Jeff arrested, but before Dane's henchman can organize a lynch mob, Fuzzy breaks him out and Jeff heads after Dane again. It doesn't take long to see Fuzzy is the best thing about this movie.

BILLY THE KID OUTLAWED (PRC, 1940): This is the first of six Billy the Kid films with Bob Steele. In Lincoln County, New Mexico, Billy the Kid and his pals (Fuzzy and Carleton Young) are outlawed by a corrupt lawman (Ted Adams) who is cahoots with local crooks who are planning a big swindle. This was a pretty fair start for the series, and Steele, Fuzzy, and Young make a nice trio and seem to enjoy working together.

THE LONE RIDER AMBUSHED (PRC, 1941): Tom Cameron (George Houston as The Lone Rider) is a dead ringer for the wanted outlaw Keno Harris (also Houston), who is responsible for money never recovered in a $100,000 robbery. Tom has the Sheriff re-jail Keno on a trumped-up charge, while he joins up with Keno's old gang in the hopes they will lead him to the money, but his plan has a couple of flaws; none of the gang knows where the money is and now expect the just-arrived Keno to lead them to it for their split; and Keno's girl, Linda (Maxine Leslie), begins to grow suspicious of Cameron, as he is nowhere near as "friendly" as Keno used to be. Plus, this Keno can sing, which Keno couldn't do before he went to jail. Fuzzy adds zest to this movie. Not a bad film; the inclusion of Fuzzy makes it better.

JESSE JAMES, JR (aka SUNDOWN FURY) (Republic, 1942): The telegraph is coming to Sundown and Amos Martin (Karl Hackett), Sam Carson), Stanley Blystone), and the crooked sheriff (Jack Kirk) are out to stop it. But Johnny Barrett (Don Barry) is there to help bring it in, and he is assisted by the bicycle-riding Pop Sawyer (Fuzzy). This may be Fuzzy's best performance in a B-Western.

LAW OF THE SADDLE (PRC, 1943): Kinney's (Lane Chandler) racket is to get elected sheriff, let his outlaw gang clean up, and then move on to another town. Rocky Cameron (Bob Livingston as the Lone Rider) is called in, and he is able to catch up with Kinney. But Kinney frames Rocky for murder, and Rocky finds himself in jail. Fuzzy provides valuable assistance to the Lone Rider.

RAIDERS OF RED GAP (PRC, 1943): Rocky (Bob Livingston as The Lone Rider) is thought to be a crook and is hired to kill off competing ranchers so one crooked rancher can nab all the cattle in the area. Of course Rocky turns the tables on him. Livingston liked Fuzzy, and they worked well together. Fuzzy was never better.

THE DEVIL RIDERS (PRC, 1943): A crooked lawyer and his gang are trying to steal some government land meant for a stagecoach company. The company hires Billy Carson (Crabbe) and Fuzzy to stop them. Buster is tough, and Fuzzy is delightful.

THUNDERING GUN SLINGERS (PRC, 1944): When Billy Carson's (Buster Crabbe) uncle is lynched, supposedly as a rustler, Billy arrives looking for the murderers. He finds that Steve Kirby (Charlie King) holds a forged note on his Uncle's ranch. When Kirby sees that Billy means trouble for him, he has Billy framed for murder. Then while Kirby is inciting the mob to lynch him, Billy's new friend Doc Jones (Fuzzy) is trying to break Billy out of jail. All is not serious as Fuzzy provides some fine humor.

WOLVES OF THE RANGE (PRC, 1943): Harry Dorn (I. Stanford Jolley) is after the rancher's land, and is trying to stop Banker Brady (Ed Cassidy) from helping them. When his man Hammond (Jack Ingram) kills Brady, there is a run on the bank. When Rocky (Bob Livingston) volunteers to ride to the next town for money, he is ambushed by Dorn's men, loses his memory, and is jailed for supposedly stealing the money. Fuzzy comes to the rescue, and also provides some funny moments.

PRAIRIE RUSTLERS (PRC, 1943): Billy Carson (Buster Crabbe) is accused of the crimes committed by his dead-ringer, outlaw cousin Jim Slade (also Buster), and barely escapes a lynching. With the aid of his old pal Fuzzy Jones, Billy catches up with his cousin, and clears his own name. Fuzzy turns in a fine performance.

FUZZY SETTLES DOWN (PRC, 1944): A sidekick's name in a film title – it never happened before or since. Wishing to settle down, Fuzzy uses his reward money to buy a newspaper. He then raises money for the new telegraph line. When the money is stolen, Barlowe (Charlie King) incites the town's people to hang him. But his pal Billy Carson (Buster Crabbe) is at work to clear him.

Of all of the B-Western sidekicks, Smiley Burnette was the only one to get top billing in a B-Western. This film should have had Al St. John with top billing in the credits. As Fuzzy Q. Jones, St. John is the title character and he has the most screen time. Buster Crabbe, as Billy Carson, is a strong hero, but he really is like a "reverse sidekick" for most of the movie.

Al St. John was usually a better actor than the lead actors he supported, and the people at PRC must have been aware of it. He absolutely knew how to entertain and draw attention to himself while on screen. This movie is his showcase. If you are a fan of Fuzzy Q. Jones, this movie spotlights his character more than usual.

WILD HORSE PHANTOM (PRC, 1945): The Link Daggett (Kermit Maynard) gang is sent to prison for bank robbery, but the bank's money is not recovered, and the ranchers face ruin. Billy Carson (Buster Crabbe), a friend of the ranchers, comes up with a plan to recover the money. Daggett and his gang are allowed to escape, and Billy and his pal Fuzzy trail them to the Wild Horse Mine. Daggett is angered and puzzled to find that the money is where he left it in the mine. Then a mysterious voice drives Daggett and his gang from the mine. Billy learns that the mine belongs to Ed Garnet (Budd Buster), an old miner who fanatically believes it contains fabulous riches. Billy's meeting with Garnet's daughter Marian (Janet Warren) leads him to Walters (Hal Price), the banker who refuses to allow the ranchers more time on their mortgage notes. Fuzzy gets spooked, and is really funny.

GANGSTER'S DEN (PRC, 1945): Lawyer Horace Black (I. Stanford Jolley) is after both Taylor's (Karl Hackett) saloon and the Lane ranch (Sydney Logan as Ruth Taylor). Fuzzy takes the gold from his and Billy's (Buster Crabbe) mine and buys Taylor's. This puts him and Billy in conflict with Black and his gang. Fuzzy buys a saloon from Karl Hackett. Along with his cook Emmett Lynn and a drunken Charlie King, we get as much comedy as we do action. This is absolutely a must see from the Buster Crabbe series.

HIS BROTHER'S GHOST (PRC, 1945): It's Fuzzy's movie all the way as he plays a dual role. Andy (Fuzzy) is ambushed by outlaws, and sends for his look-a-like brother (also Fuzzy). After Andy's death, the bad men see Fuzzy and think he Andy's ghost. Billy (Buster Crabbe) and Fuzzy break up the outlaw gang. Fuzzy shows he can do well in a dramatic role.

OUTLAWS OF THE PLAINS (PRC, 1946): A mean gang of swindlers led by Nord Finner (Charles King) take advantage of the superstitious Fuzzy by advising him through a mysterious voice, which he believes is that of a deceased Indian chief. Fuzzy persuades his fellow townsmen to join him in buying worthless property, but Billy Carson (Buster Crabbe) comes to the rescue. By this time, St. John had really refined his Fuzzy Q. Jones character.

GHOST OF HIDDEN VALLEY (PRC, 1946): Rustled cattle are being driven across the abandoned Trenton ranch, and it has acquired the reputation of a ghost ranch to keep people away. When Henry Trenton (John Meredith) arrives from England to take over the ranch, the rustlers try to get rid of him. But Billy (Buster Crabbe) and Fuzzy are on hand to help Trenton, and it's not long before they have to go into action. Naturally, the superstitious Fuzzy wants nothing to do with ghosts.

GHOST TOWN RENGADES (PRC, 1947): Gold has been found and Vance Sharp (Jack Ingram) is out to get the land. He has the landowners killed and then has Watson (William Fawcett) forge new deeds. Cheyenne (Lash LaRue) and Fuzzy arrive in time to save the land. Then they go after the gang and its leader.

Fuzzy really shines in this one. There is one funny scene when he, Lash, and Diane Trent (Jennifer Holt) spend the night in the ghost town in a room that Fuzzy thinks is full of spooks. A particularly funny part is when Fuzzy mistakes a mirror for a window, and tells Lash that one of the toughest and ugliest hombres he has ever seen is spying in the window at them. Fuzzy usually came out on top, but it was always in some humorously distorted position.

DEADMAN'S GOLD (Western Adventure/Screen/Guild, 1948): Matt Conway (John Cason) and his criminals steal a letter from the stagecoach concerning an assay report of a mine. Lash and Fuzzy arrive in Gold Valley to lend a helping hand. Lash goes after the crooks, but deduces that they are working for someone higher up. Lash and Fuzzy then set a trap to capture the killers and unmask the mastermind. There are plenty of good fist fights and whip use by Lash. The best is at the beginning when Lash whips and lassos a shot glass from a henchman's hand, and Fuzzy comments that Lash is slipping since a few drops were spilled.

OUTLAW COUNTRY (Western Adventure/Screen Guild, 1949): Marshal Clark (John Merton) sends Lash LaRue and Fuzzy out to break up a gang of counterfeiters, led by Jim McCord (Dan White), operating in a deserted village across the border. On the way, they chase off three outlaws in pursuit of a wagon carrying Frank Evans (Ted Adams) and his daughter Jane (Nancy Saunders), who are trying to escape from the outlaw hideout. Lash leaves Fuzzy to guard the buckboard while he escorts the Evans' to a friend's cabin, and returns to find Fuzzy missing and a note, signed by the Frontier Phantom, advising him to get out of

"Quiet, Lash. I'm gonna surround them."

the country. He returns to the cabin and also finds Evans and his daughter gone, but runs into the Frontier Phantom, who is his exact double and his long-lost twin brother. They fight; Lash wins and takes the Phantom's clothes and heads for the outlaw stronghold. There he finds Fuzzy has been made chief cook-and-bottle washer and janitor. McCord thinks there is something different about the Phantom and sends henchmen Turk (Steve Dunhill) and Buck (Lee Roberts) to trail him. Lash gets rid of Buck, but Turk returns to McCord's with the news of his real identity. Lash returns and is soon involved in a one-sided gun battle. Fuzzy goes for help, and encounters the real Frontier Phantom who rides to the gunfight to join his brother. This is perhaps Lash's best movie. By now, he and Fuzzy appear comfortable working with each other.

KING OF THE BULLWHIP (Western Adventure, 1950): This is really more of an essential Lash LaRue film than it is of Fuzzy, but it is certainly an essential film in the series. U. S. Marshals (Lash and Fuzzy) are summoned into a bandit-ridden territory by a local banker (Jack Holt). Since the bandit El Azote (Spanish for "The Whip") is known to wear a mask and carry a bullwhip, the local saloon owner, not knowing Lash is a lawman, hires him to impersonate the outlaw, and pull a series of hold-ups which will be blamed on El Azote. Lash intends to return the loot he acquires to its rightful owner, after he has learned the identity of El Azote, but his own identity is discovered by the gang before he can do so. There is an exciting whip scene near the movie's end.

"That's the bullet we've been looking for, Fuzz."

FUZZY'S FRIENDS

If you thought you kept seeing the same characters in the Western films with Fuzzy, you were not wrong. Many of the performers had quite a bit of dialogue including Karl Hackett, Ted Adams, Bud Osborne, Ed Cassidy, Budd Buster, I. Stanford Jolley, John Merton, Charlie King, George Chesebro, Frank Ellis, etc. But a lot of others like Wally West, George Morrell, Jack Evans, Herman Hack, Curley Dresden, Hank Bell, and Art Dillard often only appeared in crowd scenes.
I think the following number of appearances with Fuzzy should surprise and prove interesting to the readers:

Wally West – 53	Augie Gomez – 22
George Morrell – 51	John Merton – 21
Charlie King – 47	Chick Hannon – 21
Frank Ellis – 46	Jack Ingram – 21
Jack Evans – 45	Hank Bell – 21
Curley Dresden – 39	Roy Bucko – 19
Karl Hackett – 36	Frank McCarroll – 18
Steve Clark – 35	Ed Cassidy – 17
Jimmy Aubrey – 35	Sherry Tansey – 16
Tex Palmer – 35	Stanford Jolley –15
Budd Buster – 34	Reed Howes – 14
Art Dillard – 33	Tex Cooper – 13
George Chesebro – 32	Ed Peil, Sr. – 12
Carl Mathews – 31	Glenn Strange – 12
Kermit Maynard – 28	Lane Bradford – 12
Bud Osborne – 28	Victor Adamson – 12
John Cason – 26	Al Ferguson – 11
Slim Whitaker – 26	Milton Kibbee – 11
Ted Adams – 22	Dennis Moore – 10
Hal Price – 22	Cliff Taylor – 10

FUZZY IN ACTION

Thanks to John Brooker (with assistance from Richard B. Smith III), a long time fan of Westerns from England. It was not Brooker's intent to provide a complete synopsis of each film (which would be boring). He only wants fans to know how Fuzzy was featured in some of his Western films. Brooker took on the enormous task of reviewing *most* of Fuzzy's Western film work. After reading the write-ups, I think you will find them interesting and agree that he did a fantastic job. And I know everyone will enjoy the many funny quotes and antics by Fuzzy, and have a greater appreciation of him. Brooker not only tells what the movies are about, but provides quotes, antics, and often describes the kind of horse Fuzzy rode. You are sure to get some laughs from Fuzzy's quotes and his antics.

THE OKLAHOMA CYCLONE (Tiffany, 1930): Although he wasn't billed as Al "Fuzzy" St. John until 1941, work started on the character as early as 1930 when Al co-starred as Bob Steele's sidekick Slim in this film. In this movie, he introduced mannerisms and characteristics that would be closely associated with his Fuzzy Q. Jones role some 10 years later. His beard is little more than thick stubble – a work in progress. Over the next five years, he is listed in 15 B-Westerns in which he appears as a sidekick to Steele, Tom Tyler, "Big Boy" Williams and Rex Bell, and in a variety of roles, including henchmen, a tattooer, a drunk, and a jailbird in three Hopalong Cassidys and others.

ANTICS: chews tobacco and spits and smokes. He also sings unaccompanied. At the end of the movie, he dies in Steele's arms.

RIDERS OF THE DESERT (Monogram, 1932): Ranger Bob Steele and sidekick Fuzzy track down the Hash Knife Brooks stage robbing gang after they murder two of Bob's colleagues. The movie is well remembered as the one in which St. John kills Gabby Hayes.

QUOTES:
1. Ranger Captain Horace B. Carpenter: "What will your wife say?"
   Fuzzy: "The wife will be tickled to death. And if ticklin' don't do it, I'll try somethin' else."
2. Fuzzy's wife Louise Carver: "I'm tired of you leavin' me. You ungrateful brute - all I've done for you. No doubt you're going out with one of your nice lady friends playin' poker and leaving me here alone unprotected. If you leave me here tonight you won't find me here when you come back".
   Fuzzy: "Well, now I know I'm going."

RIDERS OF DESTINY (Monogram, 1933): Fuzzy is 5th billed in the cast, and goes to six locations for the John Wayne starrer, the movie cowboy's 1st one for Monogram/Lone Star. As the character named "Bert," Fuzzy is seen at Angeles National Forest, Palmdale, Lancaster, Hickson Ranch (later Monogram Ranch, then Gene Autry's Melody Ranch) Jauregui Ranch, and Walker Ranch.

ANTICS: He climbs up an embankment with pal Heinie Conklin, and fires his gun at escaping Wayne ("Singin' Sandy"). As a gang member, Fuzzy works for crooked land/water agent Forrest Taylor who wants the George Hayes/Cecelia Parker ranch. As a stagecoach driver, Fuzzy shouts at escaping horsewoman Cecelia Parker who has stolen money. He has short hair here and a three-day beard (or it's black makeup smeared on). Fuzzy does a combination comedy/serious part. Fuzzy employs his early habits in the B-Westerns such as tilting his hat forward with his right hand for scratching his head, side bending both legs before stepping off a porch or sidewalk, etc.

THE LAW OF THE 45s (Beacon, 1935): It's based on a William Colt MacDonald Three Mesquiteers story but there is no mention of them in the movie. "Big Boy" Williams is Tucson Smith, but Al is Stoney Martin rather than Brooke, and there is no third lead. They are cattlemen.

ANTICS: includes chewing tobacco, scratching his beard and smoking. There's no slapstick, but he sings unconvincingly with Glenn Strange's group around a campfire. He is shot in the back but recovers.

QUOTE: "A wolf is a gentleman – he always howls to let you know he's coming."

WEST OF NEVADA (Colony, 1936): Al is Rex Bell's sidekick Walla Walla Wiggins. They are on a secret mission to discover who is stealing gold off the Indian reservation.

ANTICS: He has light a beard, chews tobacco and spits, sings unaccompanied to his "love" Georgia O'Dell, and has a couple of slapstick falls. A rare visit to Lone Pine for St. John – Corriganville, Iverson Ranch and the Walker Ranch were the regular locations for his PRC Westerns. Rex Bell calls him "a windbag" and a "singing romeo."

QUOTES:
1. "Taxidermist? That's a new kind of critter on me."
2. "All my life I've searched for love and now I've found it I can't even get acquainted."
3. "Stand still or you'll be horizontal permanent."
4. Fuzzy complains about lack of food – when asked to unload a wagon he looks at his stomach and says: "Loading's what I'm interested in."

THE ROAMING COWBOY (Spectrum, 1937): Al introduces his Fuzzy character as sidekick to Fred Scott. The pair foils the plans of a banker after a ranch for its water. Al has a light beard. Fred calls him "an old warhorse" and "an old Gila monster."

ANTICS: roll your own cigarette routine, chews, and shows his dislike of women (Gabby Hayes style); boasts about fighting 10 – 12 men, but there was only one; a couple of pratfalls; introduces his wobbly legs routine; "plays" guitar and sings with Fred.

QUOTE: "You're always sticking my nose into trouble."

MELODY OF THE PLAINS (Spectrum, 1937): Fuzzy and Fred Scott are trail herders battling to save the Langley family's cattle. Slightly more beard in this one, wears chaps.

ANTICS: "plays" guitar, quick roll cigarette, forward flip with guitar round his neck; chews, spits on hands before fight. He's called "old maverick" by Fred.

QUOTES:
1. "I'm gonna find me a hole, and crawl in it for the rest of the winter."
2. "I could eat a cow – hide and all. If I'm going to be pushing up daisies, I want to do it on a full stomach."
3. On breaking up an artichoke – "must be a water lily".
4. "I'll be a tarantula's uncle."

SING COWBOY SING (Grand National, 1937): Al is Tex Ritter's sidekick Duke Evans. They thwart a gang after a girl's freight contract. Al describes himself as a 'mandolin picker' and 'accompanies' Tex, joining in the singing on one number. He's got more hair in his beard in this one and wears chaps.

ANTICS: chews, scratches his beard: falls asleep on a hitching rail; introduces the slapstick piece where he goes to lean on something, misses and falls over.

QUOTE: "I'm so tired I could go to sleep standing up."

MOONLIGHT ON THE RANGE (Spectrum, 1937): Fuzzy (lighter beard) "plays" guitar and sings with Fred who is on the trail of his villainous look-a-like brother. Fred gives Fuzzy singing lessons.

ANTICS: tumbles over after fast dismount, blows up a fountain of water, and springs Fred from jail by sawing through floorboards while Fred sings.

QUOTES:
1. "I take a bath every month," and Fred adds, "whether you need it or not."
2. After Fred and Lois January ignore him – "Pardon me, there's a fella over there I don't know."
3. Frank LaRue: "I wish Fuzzy would learn to sing or strangle to death."

THE FIGHTING DEPUTY (Spectrum, 1937): Fuzzy (lighter beard) and Fred are deputies. Fuzzy wears chaps.

ANTICS: He eats a pie and says it's cinnamon; when asked to spell cinnamon he tries but then says it's apple instead; a vegetable fight; routine with girl when she swoons after he tells her he wants to marry her; he kisses girl who shouts "Oh Ma" and runs off. Girl tells Fuzzy he's "absolutely mediocre."

QUOTE: "Me in love? Say, I know better. Woman is, was, were and are trouble."

A LAWMAN IS BORN (Republic, 1937): Among his co-starring roles in 1937, Fuzzy had a nice little cameo with Johnny Mack Brown as general store owner Eli Root. Fuzzy wore glasses in this one.

THE RANGERS' ROUNDUP (Spectrum, 1938): Fuzzy is a handyman with a medicine show who pals up with Ranger Fred.

ANTICS: During one of Fred's songs, Fuzzy dances round and falls on the campfire; comedy routine with Jimmy Aubrey as a drunk; extended routine of Fuzzy trying to get a bottle of booze for free in the saloon; has pipe shot out of his mouth during Fred's stage show.

QUOTES:
1. "Twice nothing is still nothing."
2. "I've been missed by better shots than them coyotes."
3. Answering the question "Can the Doc be trusted?" Fuzzy says, "With anything but your health."

KNIGHT OF THE PLAINS (Spectrum, 1938): Fuzzy and Fred are cattlemen out to expose a phony Spanish land grant. Fuzzy has medium beard.

ANTICS: goes cross-eyed playing with a metal puzzle; falls over after a fast dismount; a head-over-heels fall; falls flat on his face in a cream pie; "accompanies" Fred on guitar.

QUOTES:
1. Fred says: "Fuzzy goes loco when he sees food." Fuzzy, "I'm so hungry I could eat a steer on the hoof," and Fred tells him: "You eat up all the profits."
2. When asked if a shooting was an accident, Fuzzy says, "No, it was downright carelessness; he ran into a rustler when he wasn't ready to shoot."

SONGS AND BULLETS (Spectrum, 1938): He's Fuzzy Martin, the sidekick to Fred Scott who is after his uncle's murderer. He has medium beard.

ANTICS: "Plays" guitar and sings with Fred; combs his beard ready for intro to new schoolmarm, but Budd Buster says, "No use pardner – you can't improve that face"; dances with teacher during a Fred song; chewing; spits on hands as he jumps into a fight; trips over as he runs to Fred's rescue, but still shoots Sherry Tansey when gun goes off as he hits the floor; introduces the business, where he kicks heavies on their rears as they leave the scene. HORSE: Fuzzy starts this movie riding a horse with little or no face markings, but halfway through a chase on the Walker Ranch, he changes to a lighter horse with a flash on its nose; then the first horse re-appears in a later riding scene on the Walker Ranch. The horse with the white flash returns towards the end of the movie.

QUOTES:
1. "When I joined up with you, you promised me a lot of action, and I'm rarin' to go."
2. Fuzzy: "Don't start anything you jaspers as I like my meat raw."
3. Charles King says to him: "One more peep out of you, and I'll take you apart and see where all that fuzz comes from."

GUNSMOKE TRAIL (Monogram, 1938): Fuzzy is credited as Tip in this Jack Randall entry, but Jack calls him Fuzzy. He has a medium beard for this one which sees the two cowboys defeat John Merton's scheme to cheat Louise Stanley out of her inheritance. HORSE: It has white spot at the top of the nose and a white flash lower down.

ANTICS: Runs his fingers to and fro under his nose; chews; scratches his beard; combs his beard when he sees the girl – this continues Fuzzy's ever-changing view of women, for in some films, he doesn't like them around, and, in others, he fancies himself as a ladies' man; does a somersault as he goes to get water; pulled backwards by the shirt by Jack; slides off the back of his horse; sits on a hitch rail and falls over backwards; kicks bad guy up the hill at the movie's end.

QUOTES:
1. "I've been corresponding with a girl up in Omaha, and I'm in love" to which Jack replies: "It might be worth a trip to Omaha just to see her face … when she sees yours!"
2. (Referring to women) "Can I help it if I'm so doggone fascinating?"
3. "Detectives suspect everybody, and the one they don't suspect is the one that done the murder."
4. (After he's creased in the head) "If I didn't have such a hard head, I'd be dead."
5. "I'm as good as a dozen dead men."
6. The Sheriff (Al Bridge): "We're looking for a half breed called Loma. Have you seen him?" Randall: "We've seen nothing round here all day but a jack rabbit."
   Fuzzy: "And I don't think his name was Loma."
   Ted Adams: "The Sheriff had him rounded up, but he got away."
   Fuzzy: "Who, the jack rabbit?"

FRONTIER SCOUT (Grand National, 1938): Fuzzy as Whiney Roberts teams up with George Houston for the first time, but this time George is Wild Bill Hickok not the Lone Rider. They go to the aid of their Civil War compadre whose cattle business is facing bankruptcy because of rustlers. Fuzzy has a medium beard and describes himself as being "brave and unconquerable." Houston says he's a cross between a "terrier and a jack rabbit." And that "he's always hungry." HORSE has white spot at top of nose with long strip underneath.

ANTICS: gun twirl; chews; scratches whiskers; Houston slams a door, and window falls on Fuzzy's head.

QUOTE: Fuzzy: "If this town is so tough, it must have a saloon."

TRIGGER PALS (Grand National, 1939): Fuzzy (with medium beard) and his friends Lee Powell and Art Jarrett battle rustlers, and save their friend's ranch. He receives correspondence from a matrimonial agency, and is described as a "lovesick coyote."

ANTICS: spits; scratches beard; chews; quick roll cigarettes: he's lassoed from his horse and left swinging from a tree; comic routine trying to put "dude" woman on horse; puts his hand out to lean and lands in dude woman's arms; sits on needles, screams, and runs into Powell who knocks him down; he's described as a "mutton-headed old meddler."

QUOTES:
1. (After Fuzzy gives his theory about the rustlers - Powell to Jarrett) "He's improving – (to Fuzzy) if you keep on, you'll be half witted."
2. Fuzzy to Powell after Jarrett tells Powell he is to be foreman: "What am I going to be?"
   Powell: "A silent partner even if I have to gag you."
3. Powell (on hearing a sound): "I've got a feeling we've got company."
   Fuzzy: "Company? Hey, I've had company for an hour (scratches) unless it's this new underwear."; sings with Powell and Jarrett.
4. Fuzzy: "Women don't like anything but trouble."
5. (When Fuzzy is carrying Nina Guilbert's dog and bundles from her shopping the dog yelps): Nina says. "Are you hurting, Mitzi?"

Fuzzy: "No, but I'd like to (long pause) get rid of these bundles."

OKLAHOMA TERROR (Monogram, 1939): Fuzzy is sidekick to Jack Randall who breaks up a land swindle while searching for his father's killer. He has a light beard. HORSE: plain face with faint spot.

QUOTES:
1. Fuzzy (Explaining the fact he's always sleeping): "I like to dream – you meet some mighty nice people thataway."
2. Randall to Fuzzy: "Were you followed?"
   Fuzzy: "Me followed? Man, there ain't nothing ever follows me but women … much to my sorrow, I haven't seen one in two months."
3. Fuzzy: "We chase bandits for amusement."
4. Randall to Glenn Strange: "This is Fuzzy Glass."
   Fuzzy: "You can drop the glass and call me Fuzzy."

BILLY THE KID OUTLAWED (PRC, 1940): The first of Bob Steele's six Billy the Kid westerns see Billy, Jeff (Carleton Young), and Fuzzy (with light beard) in Lincoln County where a gang runs the region with its own gun law. HORSE: Fuzzy rides the horse he would mostly ride during the next few years at PRC. It has a long, white flash on its nose.

ANTICS: quick roll cigarette; scratches whiskers; in a saloon fight, every time he's hit and falls back on the bar, he takes a drink; falls backwards over a table; when Fuzzy's apple-bobbing, Jeff holds his head under. When he comes up, Fuzzy twists his ear and spits a fountain of water at Jeff; Fuzzy's always hungry in this one, and when he tries to steal a live chicken, Jeff says: "I told you to stay away from that chicken coop." Fuzzy: "Well, I was hungry." Later, he steals a pie, and falls flat on his face in it; he does a handstand with his head under water in the bowl; sings "Bury Me Not" around the campfire, and complains about not eating: "The grub's so low it ain't"; as Billy and Jeff ride off at the end with Fuzzy's horse, Fuzzy drops into the saddle from a tree carrying a chicken. "Boy they ought to clip their wings – they're getting mighty hard to catch."

BILLY THE KID IN TEXAS (PRC, 1940): Fuzzy has a light beard and carries a rag/handkerchief in his back pocket. He and Billy tackle the Lazy A gang that is terrorizing Corral City. HORSE: plain face with no marking.

ANTICS: chews; spits; Charles King and John Merton turn him upside down to see if he's got any money; he has alcohol poured over him, and he's thrown out of saloon by seat of his pants – he does a head over heels into the street; gun twirl; he dresses up in dress and mop cap to do chores; trips over and as he hits the ground, his gun goes off and he shoots Art Dillard. Charlie King obviously didn't have a stuntman in this film because after a saloon brawl his clothes are absolutely saturated in sweat. James Newill told John Brooker that he had a separate set of duds to change into at PRC for this reason, but perhaps it wasn't considered necessary for heavies.

TEXAS TERRORS (Republic, 1940): Fuzzy is 3rd in cast as the miner Frosty Larson in this Don Barry Republic picture.

ANTICS: kicks a heavy on the backside; he is grabbed by pants, and thrown out of store, and goes head over heels onto sidewalk; puts his hand out to lean and falls over.

QUOTE: Fuzzy: "Hot lead isn't on my diet."

BILLY THE KID's GUN JUSTICE (PRC, 1940): Billy, Jeff (Carelton Young, and Fuzzy fight a crook that re-channels water supplies so he can hold ranchers to ransom. HORSE: Fuzzy rides the horse with the full blaze.

ANTICS: spits; scratches whiskers; gun twirl; acts drunk in saloon to get in with the gang; sits on a hot stove; he is piled up with parcels and walks into a wall; has a hiccupping fit. (Al Ferguson is credited as Al Purgusan.)

QUOTES:
1. Bob Steele, after Fuzzy has dug a hole under a shack wall to help them escape from a posse, "Fuzzy, you're either a genius or a gopher."
2. Fuzzy to Charles King: "I promised never to tell this to a human being … so listen."

THE LONE RIDER RIDES ON (PRC, 1941): Fuzzy is a store owner, and meets George Houston (Tom Cameron for the first time): "Thanks for helping me stranger." HORSE: He rides the horse with the small white patch on his forehead and a white nose. Houston is after the gang that killed his parents and find them still operating a land swindle years later.

ANTICS: He has silly fight with Curley Dresden. Fuzzy opens his mouth to sing a song, and the voice that comes out is Houston's. Houston uses Fuzzy as a "puppet," and they dance together.

BILLY THE KID's RANGE WAR (PRC, 1941): A crook is trying to stop work on the completion of a new stage line road. HORSE: Fuzzy rides horse with white patch on forehead and white nose.

ANTICS: scratches whiskers; rag in back pocket; quick roll cigarette; uses a slingshot and says, "It's better than a gun any day of the week."; Billy (Bob Steele) slugs Fuzzy by mistake, and he ends up doing a headstand against a door; jumps off horse and goes flat on his face; window falls on Fuzzy at the finish; gives sheriff Ralph Peters a long yarn about being robbed in a trick to get Billy out of jail; the sheriff tells him he can't leave because of his prisoner:

QUOTE: Sheriff: "He's Billy the Kid." Fuzzy: "I don't care if he's Johnny the Old Man."

THE LONE RIDER CROSSES THE RIO (PRC, 1941): George Houston's on the trail of bank robber El Puma. HORSE: Fuzzy rides horse with white patch on his forehead but no stripe underneath.

ANTICS: Fuzzy does a "double talk" routine with Squire Perkins, rehearsing how he's going to ask for the Squire's daughter in marriage – Fuzzy plays both parts; dances with Rosalie (Roquell Verria) in the cantina; Houston and Fuzzy make a bizarre escape from a cantina, keeping the heavies at bay by throwing metal trays at them; Fuzzy bows when he meets Houston's friend Manuel (Thornton Edwards), and they crack heads; falls over during an escape; sings "Pancho The Mexican Bandit" with Houston.

QUOTE: "I'm so hungry, if I had some salt I could eat the barrel of this gun."

BILLY THE KID'S FIGHTING PALS (PRC, 1941): Billy discovers the town banker (Julio Rivero) is behind the murder of the marshal and other crimes. HORSE: Fuzzy rides horse with full blaze. This is the first film in which Fuzzy shares billing on the title card with the star. He is also billed as Al "Fuzzy" St. John in the cast list for the first time, but this would vary in following PRC films – sometimes he would revert to Al St. John in the cast list without the Fuzzy. But his inclusion on the title card was surely a sign that PRC appreciated his growing popularity as a B-Western sidekick.

ANTICS: gun twirling; he throws gun to Wally West, and it lands in his holster; falls head first over hitching rail and spins round it; puts hand out to lean and falls over; gun spinning act; scratches whiskers; rag in back pocket.

QUOTES:
 1: Billy: "You haven't got a thing to worry about – we'll be right behind you."
    Fuzzy: "Yeah, but how far?"
 2. (After Billy and Jeff rescue him from a hanging): "You sure saved me, a rope and a tree, from becoming one."
 3. Forrest Taylor, believing Fuzzy is new marshal: "We don't blame you for being careful – this is a dangerous job."
    Hal Price: "Yes, marshals don't live long in this town." Fuzzy leans back in chair and goes over backwards.
 4. Fuzzy sets and prints a page at the newspaper office, and tries to read it: "It's upside down – even a Chinaman couldn't read it." His face gets blacker with ink all over it. He looks in mirror and scares himself.
 5. Series of slapstick falls ends up with him tripping up Charles King so that he falls into jail cell. Billy enters office. Fuzzy: "It was a tough fight. He choked me till I was black in the face.
    Billy: "You're a better man than I am Uncle Tom."
 6. Billy: "Let's have a look at that tunnel (to Fuzzy still in blackface). Not you Mammy – you stay here."

THE LONE RIDER IN GHOST TOWN (PRC, 1941): Fuzzy is billed on title card. HORSE: Fuzzy rides the horse with the full blaze, but, later outside the hotel at the Brandeis Ranch, he is on a different horse with no blaze. A chase ensues, and he is back on the blaze horse; he shares a song with Houston "Cactus Joe".

ANTICS: gun twirl; he's pulled back by his pants. (About 19 minutes before the movie's end, there appears to be the sound of an airplane.)

QUOTES:
1: Houston: "Ghosts can't hurt you."
   Fuzzy: "No, but they can make you hurt yourself."
2. Houston: "While I'm gone, you stick around and take care of anybody who happens to show up."
   Fuzzy: "I'll be too busy taking care of myself."

BILLY THE KID IN SANTA FE (PRC, 1941): HORSE: the full blaze one. ANTICS: gun twirl; scratches whiskers; quick roll cigarette.

QUOTE:
Fuzzy: "Why didn't I think of that?"
Rex Lease as Jeff: "Because you've got nothing to think with."

THE LONE RIDER IN FRONTIER FURY (PRC, 1941): Fuzzy doesn't appear until 17 minutes and has little to do. HORSE: The one with the full blaze.

ANTICS: at a campfire, Fuzzy tosses a pancake, and his horse eats it; the horse goes round and round when he tries to mount it; goes to lean on a hitching rail and falls over: "First thing I'm gonna do is make that hitch rail longer."

QUOTE. "Tom's got the itchiest feet of any man I've ever known."

THE LONE RIDER AMBUSHED (PRC, 1941): HORSE: The blaze horse. Houston calls him "a Rhode Island Red answering to the name of 'Fuzzy' and a "locoed maverick."

ANTICS: Fuzzy gyps a bartender (George Chesebro) out of money for drinks by betting he can drink without swallowing – the bartender finally realizes the bet is less than the cost of the drink; feeds captured outlaws with spaghetti, and cuts it with scissors as it hangs from their mouths; Houston hits Fuzzy on the chin to stop him from calling him Tom Cameron; silly fight with George Chesebro; spits on hands before a fight; pulled back by pants; sends smoke signals. There are some good close-up riding inserts for Fuzzy, showing his prowess in the saddle.

QUOTE: (When he is questioned why he's going into the sheriff's office, he says): "To see the sheriff and remember this face – I'm coming out again."

THE APACHE KID (Republic, 1941): Although he wears his Fuzzy outfit, this is not fully-fledged sidekick role. Fuzzy is stage guard Dangle.

ANTICS: chews; scratches whiskers.

QUOTES:
1. "There's nothing like a good gun on a fine autumn day."
2. "I ain't been to a wedding since I missed my own."

BILLY THE KID WANTED (PRC, 1941): Glenn Strange billed as Glen in the cast list. HORSE: the one with full blaze. Another good film to see Fuzzy put in some hard riding in close-up running insert.

ANTICS: he makes three attempts to mount his horse before Dave O'Brien and Buster Crabbe grab him and throw him up into the saddle; spins Glenn Strange round in a chair, and is knocked down as he swings round; kicked in the rear by Strange, and goes head first into a safe; Fuzzy and Buster sing a drunken song together in a jail cell to cover the sound of O'Brien sawing through the roof to get them out; Fuzzy hit by falling wood and sawdust; gun twirl; Fuzzy tries to tell a story of how he faced 400 Indians; goes cross-eyed looking at a fly; O'Brien accidentally knocks Fuzzy head over heels, and he ends up in a head stand position.

QUOTES:
1. "I don't know why I herd with you (to Buster Crabbe and Dave O'Brien)… you're always on the go… I eat every meal with one foot in the air ready to jump. It's ruining my indigestion. If I ever get back to civilization, I'm gonna have enough sense to stay there. I'm getting gosh darn tired of living the life of a jackrabbit."
2. (When Buster's horse eats his lunch): "Hey, I'm the guy who's hungry round here."
3. Dave O'Brien to Fuzzy: "You may look like a groundhog, but you're not one at heart."
4. Fuzzy: "My constitution is plumb fed up on excitement."
5. Buster about Fuzzy: "He could make more mistakes than two ordinary men, but I'd trust him with my life."
6. Fuzzy: "You're going to give some friends of mine a square deal, or Paradise Valley will look like a jaw that's been dislocated."

THE LONE RIDER FIGHTS BACK (PRC, 1941): The film opens up with Fuzzy getting in a silly saloon fight. HORSE: the full blaze.

ANTICS: acts drunk so he can be thrown in jail and set up a bizarre and off-the-wall jailbreak to free Houston – he takes in a radio and microphone so Houston can sing a song and then speak to the sheriff and pretend he's someone else who's got the drop on him; "plays" guitar; chair smashed over his head in fight; thrown out of sheriff's office by his pants, and he does a somersault out on to the sidewalk.

QUOTES:
1. He describes himself to Dorothy Short as being "a double-barreled horned toad."
2. Uncle Joe Hawkes: "You're always acting like a Rhode Island Red."
   Fuzzy: "I'm free, white, and 21."
3. (After a silly fight with Charles King and Frank Ellis, he is thrown out of the saloon): "I must be slipping…in the old days it would have taken six to throw me out."

A MISSOURI OUTLAW (Republic, 1941): Fuzzy is a dairyman in this Don Barry entry. He has children, and they are threatened if he gives evidence against the killers.

BILLY THE KID'S ROUNDUP (PRC, 1941): John Elliott, who plays Dan Webster, is credited as John Webster, a typical PRC carelessness. HORSE: with the full blaze goes round and round when Fuzzy tries to mount and when he does get on the saddle falls off.

ANTICS: scratches whiskers; gun twirl; silly fight with Wally West which ends with Fuzzy kicking him and bringing a window down on his head; smokes a cigar; Fuzzy is left behind as sheriff of Gila Valley.

QUOTES:
1. "You know that I'm a man who craves a calm and peaceful life… how am I gonna find that trailing along with a couple of wild Indians like you and Jeff?"
2. Buster: "Everybody's bound to run into a little trouble now and then."
   Fuzzy: "Sure, but you ain't satisfied with the trouble that just comes along… you gotta go find it all over the country."
3. Buster: "What are you doing?"
   Fuzzy: "I'm going to put me up a notice for any maverick to beware of buckshot that enters these premises with felonious intent."
   Buster: "Hey, wait a minute. Where did you get that word felonious?"
   Fuzzy: "Over there in the dictionary. That book's full of words like that. Believe me, when I'm sheriff, I'm going to be able to use that word plenty."
   Buster: "Tell me how will an uneducated fella know whether he was being felonious or not?" Fuzzy: "By the number of buckshot he's got in his carcass."
4. (After hearing an outlaw's story): "Shucks, I could lie better than that with one hand tied behind my back."
   Carleton Young: "Fuzzy, that's not fair competition – after all, there's only two or three liars like you in the world."
5. (To Dennis Moore after he's been caught taking a shot at Buster): "Your chances for a long life aren't too good right now."
6. Young to Fuzzy: "I always said your folks should've drowned you when you was a pup."
7. Fuzzy: "I've always wanted to run a newspaper." Young: "How can you run a newspaper when you can't even spell?"
8. Fuzzy to thugs who have wrecked newspaper office: "Get on your knees, and pick up that alphabet – and pick it up in

alphabetical order, too."
9: Fuzzy to Joan Barclay: "Oh, I'm all right ma'am, just a mite dizzy."
Young: "Then he's feeling normal."
10. Fuzzy (after he drops type): "No good crying over a spilt alphabet."
11. Fuzzy falls while carrying too many newspapers: "I guess I should have made two trips." Joan Barclay: "I would think one trip like that would be enough."

ARIZONA TERRORS (Republic, 1942): Fuzzy is horse trader Hardtack alongside Don Barry in this land-grant swindle tale. He has a small beard. HORSE: He rides a horse with a patch on its forehead.

QUOTES:
1. Fuzzy: I'm so hungry I could eat a polecat."
2. When Fuzzy looks at a passing girl, his neck goes out of joint and Barry has to punch him in the jaw. "Give me a love tap," says Fuzzy (to put is neck straight again, a problem caused by Fuzzy having a double-jointed neck) "ever since they tried to hang me and missed." This happens a few times during the movie until the end when Barry runs a $5 bill past his face, and he straightens up without being punched.
3. Fuzzy: "Me and this saddle's getting mighty tired of each other."
4. Fuzzy to Sheriff Lee Shumway: "Someday, I'm gonna mess your clothes up, and you're gonna be in them."

ANTICS: spits on hands ready for a fight; chews; falls off ladder and puts head through a "Home Sweet Home" sign; spits tobacco juice; silly fight with Bud Osborne.

THE LONE RIDER AND THE BANDIT (PRC, 1942): Fuzzy (wearing a top hat) poses as the manager of a dude musician (George Houston) after Sheriff Smoky (Dennis Moore) sends for them to help him in his fight against the crooks cheating gold miners out of their claims. He has a small beard. HORSE: The horse with the full blaze.

ANTICS: He "plays" guitar for Houston singing "The Best Man of the West"; sings a song with Eddie Dean on guitar; picked up by seat of his pants by Houston; wearing a magician's coat, Fuzzy produces a live rabbit and chicken.

QUOTES:
1. Fuzzy to piano player Slim Andrews: "I don't like your playing – sounds like a train rolling through a barnyard."
2. Fuzzy to Glenn Strange about Houston: "He's played for all the Crown Heads of Europe – in fact we brought back some of the heads with us just as souvenirs."

BILLY THE KID TRAPPED (PRC, 1942): Fuzzy, Billy, and Jeff (Bud McTaggert) clean up Mesa City, and wipe out killers who have been impersonating them. The movie opens with the pals in jail accused of murder. HORSE: The horse with the full blaze.

ANTICS: scratches whiskers; spits chaw of tobacco at heavy; twirls gun; kicks George Chesebro's legs from under him.

QUOTES:
1. Bud McTaggart: "Fuzzy's done so much beefin' all his life he can't eat any of it."
2. Fuzzy (when he sees Budd Buster disguised as him): "Am I dreaming, or who am I?"
3. Fuzzy to Budd Buster: "Keep your hand away from that gun. Make one move, and you'll wake up playing a harp."
4. Fuzzy enters room on Budd Buster's shoulders: "Lighthorseman Jones reporting with a prisoner."
5. Fuzzy to Sheriff (Ted Adams) at the end: "Will it be all right if I use that bed (in the cell)?" Sheriff: How long?"
Fuzzy: "Six months, 24 hours a day."
Sheriff: "What for?"
Fuzzy: "Sleeping. Now that everything is quiet and peaceful, I want to make up for lost sleep."

STAGECOACH EXPRESS (Republic, 1942): Fuzzy is miner Dusty Jenkins who becomes a driver for Lynn Merrick's stage line after he loses his mine. Don Barry, his partner in the mine calls Fuzzy "a mattress-faced son of a gun."

ANTICS: smokes; does his single-handed, roll-your-own cigarette trick; chews; twirls gun; ends up in black face when he takes a photograph, the powder explodes, and he does a forward flip.

THE LONE RIDER IN CHEYENNE (PRC, 1942): When Smoky Moore is falsely accused of a bank robbery, the Lone Rider and Fuzzy rescue him from jail, and team up to smash the crooked Cheyenne city administration. HORSE: Fuzzy rides the full blaze horse.

ANTICS: somersault; goes cross-eyed when he threads a needle; slapstick routine when he tries to get the unconscious Denny Moore off the floor; goes cross-eyed and slides down wall.

QUOTES:
1. Fuzzy: "My throat feels like my name – Fuzzy."
2. Fuzzy: "I could do with some peaceful living."

JESSE JAMES, JR. aka SUNDOWN FURY (Republic, 1942): Fuzzy is Pop Sawyer, blacksmith in Sundown and known as the town joker. Sundown is set to be new telegraph terminal. However, town councilor Karl Hackett wants it in Fargo for his own end.

ANTICS: Fuzzy comes out of the saloon on his bike with a mug of beer in his hand; rides his bike into a fence, and he goes over the fence for a perfect landing; chews; spits; pratfall; somersault off his bike as it goes downhill; single-hand cigarette roll; scratches whiskers; Fuzzy's leaning gag where he puts his hand out to lean on something, misses and falls over; gets out of jail by pretending to be sick; whistles to his bike which magically comes to him like a horse; leaps over fences; falls off his bike; sneezing fit.

QUOTES:
1. Fuzzy: "Hot diggity dog."
2. Bob Kortman calls Fuzzy "an old goat."
3. Fuzzy calls the Sheriff "a snoopy old woman."

BILLY THE KID'S SMOKING GUNS (PRC, 1942): Ranchers are being driven out of Stone City by crooks led by the Sheriff (Ted Adams) and Doc Hagan (Milton Kibbe). Fuzzy opens his own emporium as ranchers are being fleeced by existing store. HORSE: The full blaze one again.

ANTICS: has a door slammed in his face a few times; kicks Slim Whittaker in face while he's lying on floor; silly fight with Bert Dillard; chews; puts spoon of beans up his nose instead of in his mouth (he's in background – possibly an ad lib); scratches whiskers; has a rag in his back pocket. Fuzzy hit by door headfirst into pot of beans.

QUOTES:
1. Fuzzy: "Sheriffs pop out from every rock."
2. Fuzzy (after being told he's sleeping in the barn): "Nothing like a bed of new mown hay."
3. Fuzzy: "That gun's got a kick like a mule" – goes cross-eyed and falls backwards.
4. Fuzzy: "I ain't scared of no man or beast."
5. Fuzzy to Joel Newfield: "I remember I fought a big grizzly with a knife bare-handed."
   Joel: "If you had a knife you weren't bare handed."
   Fuzzy: "I mean..er.. I had a knife in my bare hand."
6. Fuzzy after falling off a ladder as he puts up a sign: "Shucks I had a pet mule used to kick me every morning harder than that fall."

THE LONE RIDER IN TEXAS JUSTICE (PRC, 1942): Fuzzy and his pals Tom and Smoky (Dennis Moore) tackle cattle rustlers posing as Padres led by a woman. HORSE: plain face – no blaze.

ANTICS: roll cigarette with one hand; Tom Cameron promotes Fuzzy as a ladies' man with power over women; Tom works Fuzzy's name into the lyrics of his "Only One Rose in Texas" song; Fuzzy's drunk act; Charles Whitaker calls Fuzzy a Rhode Island Red; Fuzzy drinks Kentucky bourbon and collapses; he falls off his horse as he rides off with Smoky and Tom, and has to run to catch them.

QUOTES:
1. Fuzzy: "They say there's so much gold up there (in Klondike) that a fella can stick his face in a pan of dirt for two seconds and come up with gold fillings in his teeth."

2. Fuzzy (on seeing a lynch party): "Looks like someone's going to have throat trouble."
3. Fuzzy: (on seeing Denny Moore): "Well pickle me for a herring – if it ain't Smoky."
4. Fuzzy (about Tom Cameron): "He's got a (criminal) record as long and as wide as Death Valley. Sheriff, put him in jail and leave him there 'til he rots."
5. Fuzzy: "Men! There's two things I hate – both of them are cattle rustlers."
6. Claire Rochelle: "Oh, Fuzzy would you do me a favor?"
   Fuzzy: "For you, I'd shoot myself."
7. Fuzzy (when he hears rustling plans) "Well, stew me for a prune."
8. Tom (to Fuzzy): "Go back to the ranch and bake a cake."
   Fuzzy: "Go back to the cake and bake a ranch."

LAW AND ORDER (PRC, 1942): Fuzzy, Billy, and Jeff foil crooks trying to swindle a blind woman out of her fortune. HORSE: white patch on forehead.

ANTICS: scratches whiskers; rag in back pocket; gun twirl.

QUOTES:
1. Fuzzy (after being shot off his horse and thinking he's dying): "Well, boys, I reckon it's all over but the funeral march. On my grave, write this epitaph: He might have been a buzzard; he might have been a saint. His best pals were Billy and Jeff, and he died with no complaint." Billy and Jeff lift him up by the throat when they realize he's not even wounded.
2. Fuzzy: "I'll slave over a hot stove cooking; I'll even take in washing, but I'll be dag-nabbed if I'll stick my neck out to be hung."
3. Fuzzy (worried about Billy): "I hope he's got a rabbit foot with him."
4. Fuzzy (thinking he's responsible for Billy's death): "I'm a lowdown tadpole, a slimy worm; I'm a no-account buzzard, and I'm a sneaking coyote. Why, I ought to be put in a cage of lions and tigers and let them tear me apart bit by bit."
5. Fuzzy (to Hal Price): You know, Fatty, you oughta reduce. The best way to do that is to go on a sudden diet."

SHERIFF OF SAGE VALLEY (PRC, 1942): Sheriff Billy and deputies Fuzzy and Jeff clash with land swindlers led by Billy's double. HORSE: white patch on the forehead.
ANTICS: Maxine Leslie plays up to Fuzzy who goes all silly and bashful; scratches whiskers; rag in pocket; silly saloon fight with Kermit Maynard; kicks Bert Dillard in the face twice outside the Walker cabin; Fuzzy falls flat on his face through a door.

QUOTE: Dave O'Brien: "Oh shut up Fuzz – you're always moaning when we get in a jam."

BORDER ROUNDUP (PRC, 1942): The Lone Rider, Fuzzy and Smoky tangle with a crooked banker out to grab a gold mine. HORSE: with white patch.

ANTICS: Fuzzy has silly fight with Nick Thompson in a shack, and finishes up pinning him to a wall with bulls horns; finishes off Charles King and Stan Jolley after their fights with Tom and Smoky by kicking them in the face.

QUOTE: Fuzzy: "I guess it was a myth." Frank Ellis: "What's a myth?" Fuzzy: "A female moth."

OVERLAND STAGECOACH (PRC, 1942: Tom, Smoky, and Fuzzy foil a crook's bid to stir up war between a stage line and the incoming railroad so that he can grab the stage line for himself. Fuzzy is credited as Al "Fuzzy" St John on the title card alongside Smoky Moore under the title and Bob Livingston above the title. HORSE: Fuzzy rides horse with full blaze.

QUOTES:
1. Fuzzy: "My poor old granny… she's 82 now… can't rope as many steers as she used to."
2. Art Mix (to Glenn Strange after Fuzzy snoops around): "Do you think he saw anything?" Glenn Strange: "No – he's too dumb."
3. Fuzzy (when Smoky arrives in town): "Smoky! Well skin my hide for a parlor rug."
4. Fuzzy (after dropping a bag on Glenn Strange as he takes a bead on Smoky): "I'm so sorry I'm just an old butterfingers."
5. Fuzzy (surprised to see Tom Cameron): "Well, turn me into a jug of applejack."

6. Spoof court case with Tom Cameron as Judge: "Fuzzy Jones, as prisoner, step up to the bar. "Fuzzy: "Could I have a drink?"
   Tom: "Order!"
   Fuzzy: "A beer."
   Tom: "Order in the court."
7. Fuzzy: "I can't see to read – I hocked my glasses three years ago."
8. Fuzzy: "Mark my words! The railroad won't last long. I wouldn't ride one of those pre-hysterical monsters."
   Smoky: "Well, if you change your mind and decide to go to work for the railroad let me know." Fuzzy: "If I changed my mind? I'd have to be out of my mind to do that."

THE MYSTERIOUS RIDER (PRC, 1942): Crooks scare folks away from Laramie so they can find a gold mine owned by a man they murdered. HORSE: the full blaze.

ANTICS: chews; he is frightened, and jumps into Billy's arms; he "plays" the violin; smokes; Billy picks him up by his pants; routine with kitten under his hat making it move along and scare him; no rag in his back pocket.

QUOTES:
1. Fuzzy (sees a poster with Billy's picture on it): "I don't know why they always have to use your picture; there's nothing wrong with my face, is there?"
2. Billy: "Do you want me to answer that?"
3. Fuzzy (after he's been shot at): Now, I'll catch my death of cold – there's a bullet hole in my hat."
   Billy: "Better to have a bullet hole in your hat than a rope around your neck."
4. Fuzzy: "I wrote some poetry about that (hanging) when I was in jail. Do you wanna hear it?" Billy: "No, not on an empty stomach." Then when Fuzzy's scared by a cat.
   Billy: "I wrote a poem about that once… do you want to hear it?"
   Fuzzy: "Ah, wise-guy!"
5. Fuzzy: "Up and at 'em. That's what any American boy would say. Just like me when I was his age. Why, I remember the time I captured 500 Indians." "How many?"
   Fuzzy: "At least five."
6. Fuzzy (about a violin): "I could make that thing talk."
   Billy: "Less talk and more work, Mr. Paganini."
   Fuzzy: "Professional jealousy."
7. Fuzzy (trying to scare the heavies): "I'm the ghost of Frank Kincaid. What murdering slew-footed maverick killed me? Unbutton your yellow-livered tongues."
8. Fuzzy (when Billy appoints him justice of the peace): "Well, fry me for a mackerel."
9. Fuzzy: "Doctor told me once that tea's a little too strong for my kidneys."
10. Fuzzy: "A woman just wasn't made to listen."

OUTLAWS OF BOULDER PASS (PRC, 1942): This is the last Lone Rider with George Houston. The character name is dropped from the title and the Lone Rider song over the front credit, but it is used over end credits. Tom and Fuzzy help their old pal Smoky defeat the gang trying to grab his ranch by forcing him to pay a toll to get to water on free range. HORSE: Fuzzy rides the horse with the small white flash on the forehead.

ANTICS: Fuzzy tells Charles King the story of Little White Riding Hood, the ghost of Little Red Riding Hood; Fuzzy has a drink of water and spits it out.

QUOTES:
1. Fuzzy: "Shucks, I never did win an argument with a woman."
2. Marjorie Manners: "Can you cook?"
   Tom Cameron: "No, but he can."
   Marjorie: "Well we can only pay…"
   Tom: "That's enough." Fuzzy: "I can't work for that."
3. Fuzzy (to Lone Rider when a girl ties him to a tree, and makes him laugh hysterically as she ties the ropes): "Will you tell this female cat who I is?"

THE KID RIDES AGAIN (PRC, 1943): Billy and Fuzzy tackle a gang in Sundown that rustles cattle to drive down the value of local ranches so they can buy them up. HORSE: Fuzzy rides the horse with the full blaze.

ANTICS: silly saloon fight with Charles King which ends up with King wrapped up in a tablecloth and Fuzzy head-butting him in the stomach; King goes down and Fuzzy head-butts the wall, and his legs go wobbly; Fuzzy sits on tacks twice; Glenn Strange hits him and he does a somersault; chews; goes over backwards in a chair.

QUOTES:
1. Stan Jolley: "I'll shout for law and order till I'm black in the face." As he says this, Fuzzy finally dislodges the ink bottle that has been stuck on his finger, and the ink hits Jolley in the face.
2. Fuzzy: "They're a hair-trigger outfit. They shoot first, and then ask you what you want."
3. Fuzzy: "Ain't women peculiar?"
4. Fuzzy: "I'm as calm as a cucumber," but then shows shaking hands.
5. Fuzzy: "He (Billy) is as gentle as a lamb if they'd leave him alone."
6. Fuzzy: "If I live through this, I'll die of surprise."
7. Fuzzy: "I don't care for anything fancy in the way of a funeral, so here goes."
8. Ted Adams: "I've a good mind to arrest you as an accomplice."
   Fuzzy: "Don't flatter yourself – if you had a good mind, you wouldn't act the way you do."
9. When Fuzzy rescues Billy from jail by knocking Sheriff Ted Adams out and leaving him hanging half out of a window, Billy says: "What's the matter with him?"
   Fuzzy: "I think he's got asthma – like to sleep with his head out of a window."

WILD HORSE RUSTLERS (PRC, 1943): Nazi agents aim to destroy horses needed by the U.S. Government. Rocky Cameron and Fuzzy's friend Smoky Moore (played not by Dennis but by Lane Chandler) is impersonated by his twin brother who is a Nazi. HORSE: He rides horse with full blaze. This is Fuzzy's only modern day western.

ANTICS: cigarette-rolling routine; draws swastikas all over jail-cell walls, and tricks his way out of jail by getting the deputy to wash the signs off the wall; times are tough, so Fuzzy sweetens Rocky's coffee with a lump of sugar on the end of a piece of string, and then saves the coffee grounds; gun twirls; clicks his heels, and does a pratfall, and walks into a door.

QUOTES:
1. Fuzzy: "Well, save my whiskers for an Army mattress."
2. Fuzzy: "What are we supposed to do?"
   Rocky: "Reconnaissance."
   Fuzzy: "Did you call me a nuisance?"
3. Fuzzy: "Nazis! Saboteurs! Why, I'll blast them into a bunch of swas-tika-tikas (walks up to the camera so his face fills the screen and looks out at the audience) … and that goes for them ornery Japs, too. I'll blast their teeth into a flock of yellow tombstones."
4. Fuzzy: "Horses! I should have joined the Navy."
   Rocky: "Quiet, Admiral."
5. Fuzzy (about Nazis): "Them ornery polecats riding on good American soil, and they ain't fit to ride on a heap of garbage."
6. Frank Ellis is driving a wagon when he is stopped by Fuzzy who wants to know if he's got any sugar aboard.
   Ellis: "I tell you, I've got nothing but hay."
   Fuzzy lets him go, but then chews some of the hay: "This hay tastes like a polecat smells – he must have been sleeping in it."
7. At the close, Fuzzy enlists in the Navy, and wears an Admiral's hat: "I'm the fightingest sailor cowboy that ever rid the seven seas … Ahoy mate, hit leather … I mean the deck… we're sailing for unknown parts … ports … anchors aweigh … full steam ahead."

FUGITIVE OF THE PLAINS (PRC, 1943): Billy joins an outlaw gang in Red Rock County to clear himself of their crimes, and discovers their leader is a woman. HORSE: Fuzzy rides the horse with the full blaze.

ANTICS: Billy picks Fuzzy up by his shirt and pants, and throws him out of the sheriff's office, and he does a forward roll onto the sidewalk; smokes; silly fight with George Chesebro; kicks Carl Sepulveda and Frank Ellis in the face to knock them out; gun twirl; he keeps swinging at Billy until Billy punches him on the nose.

QUOTES:
1. Fuzzy: "I got some respect for the wolf that drags down his own meat, but the coyote that picks their bones never appealed to me none."
2. Fuzzy (sees Billy's wanted poster): "Why, them ornery critters, putting up posters like that. There ought to be a law against it."
   Billy: "That's good – a law against wanted posters."
3. Fuzzy: "I robbed the bank, and when the sheriff and his posse of 50 men rode up, I threw so much lead at them that they hightailed back."

DEATH RIDES THE RANGE (PRC, 1943): Rocky (the Lone Rider) and Fuzzy tangle with a crook that repeatedly sells the Circle C Ranch at a cheap price, and then kills the would-be owners. HORSE: Fuzzy rides horse with full blaze.

ANTICS: smokes, silly fight with Kermit Maynard, including sliding down the banister and being kicked back up again; gun twirl; silly fight with Wally West; kicks Kermit in the rear; at the finish, Fuzzy decided he's too young to settle down and run a ranch

QUOTES:
1. Fuzzy (tending to John Elliott's wounds): "Plenty of feuding where I came from. I was a regular angel of mercy. This medicine will stop you from getting an infection in that wound. It's good. Lotta alcohol in it (swigs it and makes a face). Gosh, that's good. Fever's like a snake in the grass – it sneaks up on you." (Listens to Elliott's ankle): "There's no sign of a pulse beat there at all."
2. Fuzzy (to Rocky at the end after Patti McCarthy asks Rocky to thank the Lone Rider): "The Lone Rider? That's you."
   Rocky: "Me! Are you crazy?" (Fuzzy approaches the camera, looks out at the audience, and shrugs his shoulders.)

WESTERN CYCLONE (PRC, 1943): Glenn Strange frames Billy for murder as part of his plans to take over as State Governor. HORSE: Fuzzy rides horse with full blaze.

ANTICS: Fuzzy falls off a stagecoach; slapstick falls, after being told to drop his pants during a stage holdup; blows froth off a beer; throws beer in the air, and it comes back down in the glass; kicks Lou Fulton in the rear; lassos a heavy, and gets pulled off his feet into a forward roll; knocks out a heavy, but then gets tangled up in the rope when he tries to tie the man up; he's so hungry he dives on a chicken, but misses it; smokes; he goes head-first over a mound of straw; kicks Kermit Maynard in the face to knock him out.

QUOTES:
1. Billy (to Fuzzy): "You – with the moth-eaten whiskers."
2. Fuzzy (in saloon): "My tonsils are plumb dehydrated – I think I'll stay here and soak 'em up a bit. Give me another beer."
3. Lew Fulton (to Fuzzy who's kicking up a ruckus in jail): "You quieten down fur face."
4. Fuzzy (to Billy): "I don't know why I ride herd with you. You're always on the jump – my stomach's always empty."
5. Fuzzy (to Billy): "You're sticking your head into the lion's mouth."
6. Fuzzy: "I know how to make him talk – I'm a blood brother to the Comanche."
7. Fuzzy: "I'm so hungry I could eat boot leather." (Picks up a boot): "I could fry that and make a good fillet of sole. Nah, probably give me indigestion."
8. Fuzzy: "Sometimes I can't forget I'm a white man, even when I'm dealing with a renegade like you."
9. Fuzzy (after tickling Kermit Maynard's feet to get information): "I've never seen a man so tickled to give me a confession."
10. Fuzzy (dressed as a woman): I think I'll get me a job as a female impersonator."

WOLVES OF THE RANGE (PRC, 1943): The Cattlemen's Association chief wants the ranchers' lands, and kills the banker prepared to help them. Rocky and Fuzzy are roaming cowboys. HORSE: Fuzzy rides horse with full blaze.

ANTICS: gun twirl; routine in which Fuzzy finds money hidden all over him; he falls in through a door; silly fight with Curly Dresden which shows Fuzzy's agility and includes him falling backwards over a counter and diving Dave Sharpe-style on to Dresden; in a routine with fortune teller Pasha (Charles Whitaker), he is told he is going to meet with a violent death in a couple of days, so he pays $15 for a charm to keep him safe; at the fade-out, Fuzzy is dressed in fortune teller's outfit, and Rocky calls him Pasha Q. Jones.

QUOTES:
1. Fuzzy (to Rocky): "Bullets can't do me no harm – I've got a charmed life."
2. Rocky (to Fuzzy): "Oh, stop it! The minute you show your mug in town, guns'll start popping like firecrackers."

LAW OF THE SADDLE (PRC, 1943): A crook runs for sheriff and then cleans out Oak Bluff with his gang before moving on to Kingston and pulling the same dastardly trick. HORSE: Fuzzy rides horse with full blaze.

ANTICS: scratches beard; twirls gun; one-handed cigarette roll; acts drunk; two silly fights with Frank Ellis; kicks Ellis in the rear; falls off stagecoach; Fuzzy (or double) is flung out of wagon; Jimmy Aubrey pulls Fuzzy along by his pants; his pants are threadbare, but when Rocky pulls him back by the pants, he says: "They're the only ones I've got."; gets caught in a bear trap.

QUOTES:
1. Fuzzy: (holding a nugget): "If this is what we think it is, we'd better keep it quiet."
   Frank Ellis: "That's right - don't tell a human being."
   Fuzzy: "That's why I'm telling you."
2. Fuzzy: "Stomping out outlaws is just plain duck soup for me and my partner."
3. Rocky: "Be careful."
   Fuzzy: "You know me better than that Rocky – I never took a chance in my life."
4. Fuzzy: "They're tearing the town apart."
   Rocky: "Did you try and stop them?"
   Fuzzy: "Are you kidding?"
5. Fuzzy (after Rocky pulls Frank Ellis off him to stop him pummeling Fuzzy): "It's a good thing you got here, or I would have murdered him."
6. Fuzzy: "Whenever Rocky's got a tough job to do, he generally sends for me."
   Betty Miles: "You're sort of terrific, aren't you?"
   Fuzzy: "I don't like to brag about myself, but me and Cameron have tamed some of the toughest hombres who ever straddled a horse."
   Betty: "It must be wonderful to be so brave, modest, and handsome."
7. Rocky (grabs Fuzzy by the seat of his pants to stop him from fighting Frank Ellis): "Cool down!"
8. Rocky describes Fuzzy as a "reckless daredevil" and adds: "Fuzzy doesn't really need my help – he just lets me tag along once in a while."
9. Fuzzy (to Rocky's horse): "Some of these days you're gonna be an orphan."
10. Fuzzy (about Rocky): "I don't know why the women go crazy about him. When he's around, I'm just an old suit of clothes."
11. Rocky (about Fuzzy): "Someday, I'm gonna hang him up by the whiskers and slap some sense into him."

CATTLE STAMPEDE (PRC, 1943): Billy and Fuzzy go to work at the Circle X Ranch as a range war looms. HORSE: Fuzzy rides the horse with the full blaze.

ANTICS: gun twirl; chews; Fuzzy jumps off horse, hits the ground running, and does a forward roll; Fuzzy trips over and his gun goes off accidentally, shooting a heavy.

QUOTES:
1. Hansel Warner: "I don't usually mix in to what don't concern me."
   Fuzzy: "Those who do don't live long."
2. Fuzzy: "Worry just gets you more worry."
3. Fuzzy (to Charles King): "I don't like your face."
   Billy: "Now that you mention it Fuzz, it could stand improving."
   King: "Do you think you can do anything about it?" Fuzzy (looks closely at King's face): "That front view is very bad."
   King (to Billy): "You get that monkey outta here, or I'll tear him to bits."
   Fuzzy: "Now, let me have a look at that profile. Oh, that's even worse. Yep, it seems to be a hopeless case, but I think with a little working over it could be improved."
   King: "Would you like to try it?" This leads to a very funny fight in which King keeps swinging and missing while Fuzzy pulls his hat down, kicks him in the rear, grabs his neckerchief, and swings him round. The fight appears to be unrehearsed.

THE RENEGADE (PRC, 1943): The crooked Town Mayor (Ray Bennett) of Pine Bluffs sets out to ruin local ranchers because he knows there's oil on their land. HORSE: Fuzzy rides the horse with the full blaze.

ANTICS: walks into door; headfirst jump through window into a forward roll; falls backwards over a chair; twirls gun; funny fight with Tom London in which he slams him in a door over and over again and the pair of them are in and out of a window; Fuzzy, dressed as well-to-do gentleman, falls into a puddle.

QUOTES:
1. Lois Ranson (as Fuzzy leaves to decoy the outlaws): "Fuzzy, you're an angel."
   Fuzzy: "Not yet, but maybe soon."
2. Fuzzy: "Get moving before my trigger finger starts itching."
3. Jack Rockwell (as Fuzzy breaks Billy out of jail); "You won't get away with this."
   Fuzzy: "If we don't, you won't live to talk about it."
4. Fuzzy: "I make pancakes so light that we'll have to nail your feet to the floor to keep you floating up to heaven" (before the pancake blows up into a huge balloon shape and explodes).
5. Fuzzy: "$10,000 is a man-sized piece of change."

BLAZING FRONTIER (PRC, 1943): Two railroad men swindle ranchers out of their land so they can get rich when the rails come through. HORSE: Fuzzy rides horse with full blaze.

ANTICS: chews; so nervous from robbing a stagecoach that his he starts shaking, his legs wobbling and he falls flat on his face; twirls gun; Billy calls Fuzzy "Killer"; Fuzzy appointed a deputy by crooks; Fuzzy rips cigar out of Stan Jolley's mouth, has a drag and chokes and sticks it back in Jolley's mouth; saloon girl cuddles up to Fuzzy while she puts her hand into his pocket to rob him, but her hand gets caught in a mousetrap; single-handed cigarette roll: his clothes are blown off when he throws a cigarette into a powder keg; Fuzzy lassos Stan Jolley off his horse near the film's end.

QUOTES:
1. Fuzzy: "I'm so tough the last rattlesnake I bit just crawled away and died."
2. Fuzzy (after Billy tells him he has to rob a stagecoach to convince the heavies that he's tough): "You want me to rob a stagecoach?"
   Billy: "I'll be there to back you up."
   Fuzzy: "How far back?" Billy: "Right back."
   Fuzzy: "Well, back or front I ain't gonna be there."
3. Saloon girl (playing with Fuzzy's whiskers): "You are mucho caballero grandee, no?"
   Fuzzy: "Never mind that Spanish business – you're just plain Rosie O'Grady to me."
   Girl: "Flanagan to you."
4. Fuzzy (after shooting the letters FQJ into wood work in the saloon): "I always leave my calling card. FQJ stands for TNT. Dynamite Jones – that's what they call me."
5. Fuzzy (posing as an explosives expert): "When I blow up things, they stay blowed. Powdermonkey Jones they call me."

RAIDERS OF RED GAP (PRC, 1943): A crooked cattle company runs settlers off their land, so they can set up a meat-packing business and sell beef at top prices. HORSE: Fuzzy rides horse with full blaze.

ANTICS: Fuzzy's clothes are stolen while he sleeps out on the range, and he has to wear the thief's dude duds; legs wobble; twirls gun; Fuzzy and Rocky pose as gunmen Butch and his pal Deadpan; Fuzzy combs his beard; puts a fork full of food into his eye; Fuzzy ends up with two black eyes after a scrap with the sheriff.

QUOTES:
1. Rocky (when Fuzzy eats food from Myrna Dell's lunch basket): Don't be a pig, you pig. (Grabs food and starts eating it) What's the matter with you?"
2. Myrna Dell (about Fuzzy): "He looks as though he's just escaped from the circus... or worse."
3. Fuzzy: "I'm hungry enough to eat a horse."
   Rocky: "Well, go ahead, you've got one."
   Fuzzy: "Yeah, but if I did that, I'd have to walk, and I don't like walking."
4. Sheriff George Chesebro (to Fuzzy): "Don't get excited. Jail ain't so bad – it's the hanging that hurts."
5. Kermit Maynard (to Fuzzy): "Save your breath, or you ain't gonna have any to spare."
6. Fuzzy (enjoying being looked after in jail): "I know my rights. I'm a prisoner. and I'm gonna stay a prisoner"… (to Rocky)

"I know when I'm well off - I'm eating three times a day, sleep like a baby and no work – so run away little boy, and don't bother me."

DEVIL RIDERS (PRC, 1943): Crooks in Mesa City stir up a feud between friendly rivals — the Pony Express and the Farrell (Frank LaRue) stage line. Fuzzy is a blacksmith with the Pony Express. HORSE: Fuzzy rides the horse with the full blaze.

ANTICS: sits on a hot horseshoe, and then sits in a horse trough to cool down; at a dance, Fuzzy goes into a comedy-dance routine which includes his wobbly legs, a forward roll, cartwheels, and his leaning gag; he dances with a woman, spinning her around until she almost goes out of a window; Charles King chops Fuzzy on the neck, and he does a forward flip.

QUOTES:
1. Fuzzy: "I'd fight anybody, any time, any place."
2. Billy (after Fuzzy crashes through window with couple of horseshoes attached to the seat of his pants): "That's the first time I heard of a horse shoeing a man."

FRONTIER OUTLAWS (PRC, 1944): Crooks engineer a land grab in the Wolf Valley area. HORSE: Fuzzy rides horse with full blaze. The Range Busters' "Home on the Range" music is used over start-and-end credits.

ANTICS: silly saloon fight with Ray Henderson, head-butting him in the stomach, throwing him over the bar, kicking him on the rear, and hitting him over the head with a bottle; rag in back pocket; scratches whiskers.

QUOTES:
1. Fuzzy (he cracks window down on Charles King's head and KO's him): "He talks too much."
2. Billy: "I'm not gonna be kept on the run."
   Fuzzy: "Doctor told me running was bad for my constitution, too."
3. Fuzzy (when he's confronted by Marin Sais with a rifle): "You might as well shoot me as scare me to death, Ma."
4. Fuzzy (to Marin Sais) "Remember, I ain't a marrying man."
5. Fuzzy (to stage driver after taking money off stage): "Now, spank your ponies outta here."
6. Fuzzy: "I was looking for you no place, and found you everywhere."

THUNDERING GUN SLINGERS (PRC, 1944): When his uncle is hanged on a trumped-up rustling charge, Billy goes gunning for justice. It's unusual, because in this film Billy and Fuzzy don't know each other. Fuzzy is a horse doctor who also treats humans. HORSE: he rides horse with the full blaze.

ANTICS: Billy calls Fuzzy "fur face"; Fuzzy's legs wobble when he's pulled off his horse; Billy tries to help Fuzzy into the saddle, but throws him right over it and onto the ground; Billy massages Fuzzy's back with horse liniment; slapstick saloon fight; Fuzzy runs through a door, and trips over Kermit Maynard on the floor; Charles King calls Fuzzy a "gabby horse doctor"; drink-swapping routine with Budd Buster.

QUOTES:
1. Fuzzy tries to treat a mule that's supposedly been bitten by a rattlesnake. He listens with a stethoscope, takes the mule's pulse by holding up a front leg, tries to lift the mule up when it sits down and then gets thrown across his office when he tries to sit on its back, and is spun round and round: "You'd better fetch the rattler that bit him – he needs a doctor more than this ornery mule does."
2. Fuzzy (after being told off by Budd Buster for getting involved in saloon brawl): "Steve Kirby insulted my intelligence." Buster: "That wasn't much to fight about."
3. Fuzzy: "There are a lot of things around here I don't like the smell of; it's about time somebody did some fumigating."
4. Fuzzy: "I'm fed up of picking bullets outta people."
5. Fuzzy (to Budd Buster): "I'd rather have a rattlesnake inside me than an ossified liver."
6. Fuzzy (as Billy and King fight it out at the saloon, and a mob moves in): "It's a private confabulation, and they don't wanna be disturbed."

VALLEY OF VENGEANCE (PRC, 1944): UK title: VENGEANCE. Years after their parents are murdered in an ambush, Billy and Fuzzy get together to bring the killers to justice. David Polanski plays Fuzzy as a boy, but why he would be called Fuzzy from such a young age is anybody's guess. HORSE: Fuzzy rides the horse with the full blaze. PRC's earlier "cap gun" sounds are replaced in this film with a more solid sound effect.

ANTICS: Fuzzy is an explosions, and, ammunition expert; rag in back pocket; silly fight with John Merton in which he head butts him in the stomach, and lands uppercuts to his jaw to KO him; Billy and Fuzzy hug each other when they meet up again after so many years; Steve Clark calls Fuzzy "a hairy ape."

THE DRIFTER (PRC, 1944): Billy's exact double Drifter Davis is impersonating Billy so he will get the blame for a series of bank robberies. HORSE: Fuzzy rides the horse with the full blaze. There's little action in this one – a tiresome entry.

ANTICS: various bits of slapstick action see Fuzzy being tripped, hit and thrown around; single-handed cigarette roll; confused by the continuous switching between Billy and Drifter, Fuzzy puts in ear plugs so he can't hear Billy tell him who he is; Fuzzy kicks Jimmy Aubrey in the rear.

QUOTES:
1. Roy Brent (about Fuzzy): "He looks like a Rhode Island Red, and acts like a disappointed mountain goat, but he walks something like a man."
2. Fuzzy (to Jimmy Aubrey): "I'm one of the best lassoers in the country."
3. Fuzzy: "If I make any more mistakes around here, I won't be riding a horse, I'll be flapping wings and flying."
4. Fuzzy: "Two birds in the hand is worth one in the sagebrush."
5. Billy (to Fuzzy): "I've met a lot of dumb, stubborn, stupid, hot-headed mules in my time, but you're the most self-centered and senseless one I ever met."
6. Fuzzy: "I can make that thing (his bicycle) jump through hoops." He whistles and the bike stands up, and goes over to him. He calls it Fuzzy Q. Jones, Jr., and does a few tricks on it.

FUZZY SETTLES DOWN (PRC, 1944): Billy and Fuzzy take control of a newspaper, and help the locals get the telegraph into Red Rock. HORSE: Fuzzy rides horse with full blaze.

ANTICS: Fuzzy is flattened by robbers running out of a bank; he scares himself looking in a window and seeing his own reflection; chews; rag in back pocket; drinks a beer; John Merton throws an egg at Fuzzy; silly fight with Frank McCarroll; catches fingers in printing press; ends the film wearing top hat and tails, but when Billy rides off, he gives the newspaper away, he rides after him.

QUOTES:
1. Fuzzy: "I'm all death and destruction when I get riled."
2. Fuzzy: "I'm getting tired eating trail dust all the time – I'd like to find a nice peaceable spot and take root."
3. Billy (as Fuzzy licks thumbs to count reward money): "You wanna stop counting that money, Fuzz? You'll wear it out."
   Fuzzy: "I'll stop when it starts to look frayed."
4. Fuzzy: "I've always hankered to be somebody, wear good clothes, so when I walk down the street people will turn to me, bow, and say Howdy, Mr. Jones. (he yells this out because as he bows, his rear is burned by the campfire.)
5. Fuzzy: "You talk as though I've got no intelligence."
   Billy: "Where you been hiding it all these years?"
6. Billy (after Fuzzy buys a newspaper): "I hope you won't forget your friends now that you're so important."
   Fuzzy: "Get away boy, you bother me."
7. Fuzzy: "I'd like to lay my hands on those fellas. Who were they?"
   Billy: "I don't know but they looked familiar."
   Fuzzy: "If I get hold of them, they won't look familiar even to their mother."
8. Fuzzy (to Patti McCarty after Billy gets his lunch): What am I supposed to live on – flowers and sunshine?"
9. Billy (after Fuzzy spills ink over ranchers' money): "If that's the only dirty money you ever handle, you'll be doing all right."

WILD HORSE PHANTOM (PRC, 1944): Bank robbers are allowed to escape from jail so they can lead Billy to where they hid the money so he can help the Piedmont Valley ranchers avoid foreclosures on their land. HORSE: Fuzzy rides horse with full blaze. Unlike in a lot of the Autry pictures, it is unusual for the Crabbe/St John Westerns to feature cars.

ANTICS: Fuzzy dabs tears from his eyes when his young cousin dies; at the sound of ghostly laughter, Fuzzy jumps on Billy's back; Fuzzy attacked by a giant bat (a prop from the movie DEVIL BAT (PRC, 1941); Billy pulls him back by his pants;

Fuzzy's so scared, he yells out but, no sound comes out; silly fight with Frank McCarroll, head butting him in the stomach and uppercuts to the jaw; kicks him in the rear; Fuzzy runs amok, and jumps into people, over tables, and up a wall – he's got a "baby bat" inside his shirt; he faints into Billy's arms.

QUOTES:
1. Fuzzy: "Outlaw is just another word for fool."
2. Billy (in "ghost" mine): "Be quiet, Fuzzy and stay close to me."
   Fuzzy: "If I get any closer, I'll be in your hip pocket."
3. Fuzzy: "I've got cats' eyes – I can see anything" (before he falls headfirst into an ore bucket).
4. Fuzzy: "Don't worry, Billy, I'll get you out of this."
   Billy: "Like you got me into it?"
5. Fuzzy: "Go ahead, I'm behind you."
   Billy: "How far?"

OATH OF VENGEANCE (PRC, 1944): Crooks stir up a feud between ranchers and settlers, and store owner Fuzzy calls in Billy to help. HORSE: Fuzzy rides horse with full blaze.

ANTICS: Fuzzy throws a calf, after a slapstick routine, but he catches his foot in the rope, and the calf drags him along through the dirt; wobbly legs; stands on a rake which comes up and hits him in the back; he's "fed up with cattle," so he opens a general store; catches hand in a mouse-trap; slapstick fight with Frank Ellis; spits on hands before a fight; sits on a cactus; trips over sidewalk; silly fight with Jack Ingram; licks pencil before writing;

QUOTES:
1. Billy (lifting Fuzzy up by his handkerchief): "You're sure a wildcat when you get riled, Fuzz."
2. Fuzzy: "I don't know what can plague a man worse – a woman or a mosquito."
3. Mady Lawrence: "You bewhiskered old goat – you'll find yourself heading down the road so fast they'll be playing checkers on your coat tails."
4. Jack Ingram (to Fuzzy): "If you're so afraid of a little trouble, why don't you find a nice gopher hole and crawl in it?"
5. Fuzzy: "Women ought to stay at home when a man's got work to do."
6. Marin Sais (about Fuzzy's head): "No sense – no feeling."
7. Billy (to Fuzzy): "You always do it the hard way." (This is a running gag throughout the film.)
8. Billy: "You can't open your mouth without putting your foot in it."
9. Marin Sais (to Fuzzy): "I think I'll marry you."
   Fuzzy (ducking out of her clutches): "Oh no, you won't." (Then he tells Billy to sell his store or give it away, and he runs out of town.)

LIGHTNING RAIDERS (PRC, 1945): Hayden (Steve Darrell) lends money to the ranchers, and then robs the stage that's bringing the money they were relying on to pay him back. HORSE: Fuzzy rides a darker horse than usual – it has a small white mark on its forehead.

ANTICS: Fuzzy eats Mexican jumping beans, which leads to a crazy slapstick scene with him jumping all over the place; in saloon brawl, Stan Jolley swings at Billy, but hits Fuzzy instead; walks into a wall; silly fight with Frank Ellis; twirls gun; Fuzzy licks fingers to count money.

QUOTES:
1. Fuzzy (about the sheriff): "He couldn't catch a fly in a bucket."
2. Fuzzy: "Doggone mail robbers are lower than lizards – they're hyenas."
3. Fuzzy: "I'm a ferret when it comes to finding out things."
4. Billy (after hearing one of Fuzzy's ideas): "Now you're using your head for something else besides growing whiskers."
5. Fuzzy: "I'm going to stick so close to you that they'll think I'm your twin."
   Billy: "Don't wish that on me."
6. Fuzzy jumps into Billy's arms: "It's those jumping beans – they must be multiplying."
   Billy: "If they are, I'm gonna have to buy you an anchor."
7. Billy: "That's a fine mess you got us into Fuzzy."
8. Mady Lawrence kisses Fuzzy.
   Billy (to Fuzzy): "You're blushing" (then Fuzzy falls flat on his face).

HIS BROTHER'S GHOST (PRC, 1945): Fuzzy has a dual role. Thorne (Charlie King) and his gang are wiping out the ranchers because they know the railroad is coming through, and that a flood of new settlers will be eager to buy land. When they kill the sharecroppers' champion Andy Jones, Billy Carson has Fuzzy (Andy's brother), a sheepherder, become Andy's ghost to help him round up the gang. HORSE: The one with the full blaze.

ANTICS: in a bizarre trick scene, Fuzzy's head appears from behind a narrow post; rag in back pocket; Fuzzy rises up in a sheet as a "ghost" to scare Karl Hackett; Charles King hits Fuzzy and he falls out of a window; kicks Carl Mathews in the rear.

QUOTES:
1. Billy: "Are you hurt bad?"
   Andy: "No, you dang fool, I'm making mud pies."
2. Andy (to Billy): "I'm a man. There ain't a bullet big enough to kill me."
3. Doc Karl Hackett (to Andy in death bed scene): "Maybe you'll never die like ordinary mortal; Maybe you'll fool us."
4. Andy (to Billy): "Send for my brother Jonathan. He's about my size... the dang little runt. Never amounted to a hill of beans."
5. Billy (to Fuzzy): "You're Jonathan, aren't you?"
   Fuzzy: "I reckon I did travel with that handle at one time, but where I come from, they call me Fuzzy."
6. Fuzzy: "You'd better talk, or that mug of yours is gonna look like a spoilt custard pie."
7. Fuzzy (to Arch Hall): "Now drop that gun before I send you where you belong."

SHADOWS OF DEATH (PRC, 1945): Landreau (Charlie King) wants the ranchers' land around Red Rock because the railroad's coming through. Fuzzy, who is the town's justice of the peace, marshal, and barber, sends for Billy Carson.

ANTICS: Fuzzy kicks Jimmy Aubrey in the rear; comic-shaving scene with Bud Osborne; slips on soap; switches from being a barber to a marshal and to a justice of the peace in quick succession by changing clothes; silly fight with Frank Ellis with Fuzzy at one point sitting on his shoulders; Fuzzy appears to be cutting hair, but a bald man slips out from under his toupee to get a cigar while Fuzzy continues cutting; Billy throws Fuzzy out of the saloon; comedy routine where Fuzzy drops a razor blade down the back of Frank Ellis; silly fight with Ellis; Fuzzy trips over and shoots John Cason; long barbershop routine with Fuzzy cutting Budd Buster's beard.

QUOTES:
1. King (to Fuzzy): "For a little man, you open your mouth too wide."
2. Billy (after Fuzzy's been thrown out on the sidewalk twice): "Don't you get tired doing that?" Fuzzy: "No, it's my way of working up an appetite."
3. Fuzzy (to Emmett Lynn who's having a bath in his barbershop): "Scrub yourself and get out… don't hang around like a hippopotamus. And next time you take a bath, put your spurs on." Emmett: "You just said that on the spur of the moment, didn't you?"
4. Billy: "Hey, Fuzz, what do you do in your spare time?"
   Fuzzy: "I'm a doctor."
   Billy: "A what?" Fuzzy: "A horse doctor."
5. Donna Dax: "My horse lost a shoe – would you fix it for me?"
   Fuzzy: "I'm a pretty busy man – even if I was twins, there wouldn't be enough of me."
6. Fuzzy (in saloon): "Give me a big tall (looks down at his marshal's badge)… sarsaparilla."
7. Fuzzy in justice of the peace clothes (to Donna Dax and Eddie Hall at the finish): "You're charged with intent to commit matrimony. Guilty or not guilty?"
   Donna and Eddie: "Guilty."
   Fuzzy (to the audience as he prepares to marry them): "Ain't this a cute way to finish a story?"

GANGSTER'S DEN (PRC, 1945): Fuzzy buys a saloon, but Lawyer Black (I. Stanford Jolley) wants it and a nearby ranch because he's discovered that gold runs underneath the properties. HORSE: Fuzzy rides horse with full blaze.

ANTICS: Fuzzy climbs in a tree, off his horse, when bullets start flying; leaps into the saddle and goes right over the horse; rag in back pocket; Fuzzy uses a mop to hit heavies in saloon brawl; he strikes a match on his whiskers; silly fight with Stan Jolley.

QUOTES:
1. Fuzzy: "I crave action and excitement."

2. Fuzzy (tosses a flapjack which comes down and hits him on the head, making him cross-eyed): "That does it. When I lose my touch with flapjacks, it's time for a change of scenery."
3. Fuzzy: I'm going into town with the boys. The way I feel right now, I'll set them an example that'll shame them into staying sober."
4. Fuzzy: "That Taylor (Karl Hackett) place (saloon) has gotta be run out of business."
   Billy: "Thinking of drinking it dry, Fuzz?"
5. Fuzzy (to heroine Sydney Logan): "By the way, the next time you do any shooting, you call your shots – I haven't had time to look yet, but I think I'm packing some of your lead."
6. Fuzzy: "I'm going to give him a piece of my mind."
   Billy: "You better take it easy – you haven't got much to spare."
7. Fuzzy to Emmett Lynn: "You wear this thing (chef's hat) – then maybe you can cook better." Lynn: "I'll quit before I wear this thing – it makes my head hot."
   Fuzzy: "Then fry an egg on it."
8. Charles King (in one of his comic roles): "I like this place (the saloon) –how about giving me a job?"
   Fuzzy: "You're big enough and ugly enough."
   King: "I was a pretty baby."
   Fuzzy: "Something must have went wrong."
9. Fuzzy takes King on as his bodyguard ,but bumps heads with him: "Why don't you get outta my way?"
   King: "How can I get outta your way and guard your body?"
   Fuzzy: "You don't have to stand that close."

STAGECOACH OUTLAWS (PRC, 1945): Kirby (I. Stanford Jolley) wants the Bowen (Ed Cassidy) freight business, and calls in a convicted killer to back his play. Fuzzy is mistaken for the killer. HORSE: with full blaze.

ANTICS: twirls gun; shoots the end off Jimmy Aubrey's cigar; trips over broken hitch rail; his gun shakes as he prepares to rob stage; pulled back by the pants by Billy; trips over body; GOOF: when Herman Hack runs into room where Fuzzy is at the crooks hideout, he pulls his gun out before he opens the door but when he enters the room his hand is empty and he has to go for his gun again; Fuzzy kicks Hack in the rear.

QUOTES:
1. Sheriff Steve Clark calls Fuzzy "an ossified idiot": "You haven't got enough brains to fill a thimble."
2. Billy (to Fuzzy as Matt Brawley): "I mistook you for a scatter-brained maverick named Fuzzy Jones. He hasn't got enough sense to come in out of the rain. Generally up to his ears in a mess of trouble."
3. John Cason raises a drink: "Here's how."
   Fuzzy: "I know how."
4. Fuzzy (to Kermit Maynard): "Do I look half-wit?" (to John Cason): "Don't you answer that."
5. Fuzzy: "I'm in a good spot to get my head shot off."
   Billy: "What's the difference? You never use it for anything."
   Fuzzy: "I've gottta have some place to hang my hat."
6. Fuzzy: "I'm making tracks for Cherokee. It's not much of a town, but I'd rather be alive there than dead any place else."
7. Fuzzy (as crooks try to barge past him out of the sheriff's office): "Get back there before I cloud up and snow all over you."
8. Fuzzy: "Night is just like daylight, but a bit darker."
9. Fuzzy: "I'm just wasting my time here in Cherokee. I should go some place where I could spread out and become important." Bob Kortman then KOs him with a punch.
   Billy: "He sure spread out in a hurry." Puts Fuzzy over his shoulder and leaves, saying to Steve Clark: "I'll let you know if he ever gets to be important."

RUSTLERS HIDEOUT (PRC, 1945): A saloon owner and a banker rustle an honest rancher's cattle so they can put him out of business and grab his land and packing company. HORSE: Fuzzy rides horse with full blaze.

ANTICS: Fuzzy pulled back by his pants by Billy; he is knocked over several times by flying bodies in saloon brawl; licks fingers quickly when he counts money; he carries a hog-tied Al Ferguson in at the finish, and then faints and falls flat on his face; kicks Osborne in the rear. GOOF: Crabbe is named Billy Gibson not Carson in title credits.

QUOTES:
1. Billy: "Right now, I'm as hungry as you always are."

2. Billy (gives Fuzzy a dollar bill): "This is what you get for your worrying."
   Fuzzy: "Didn't do much worrying, did I?"
3. Fuzzy (counting out dollars for Billy): "One for you… one for me… two for you… one two for me… three for you… one two three for me… four for you… one two three four for me…"
4. Billy (to Bud Osborne): "Who hired you to stampede those cattle?"
   Fuzzy: "Talk and talk fast."
   Osborne: "You're both wasting your time."
   Fuzzy: "You won't have any to waste when we get through with you."
5. Fuzzy: "I've been sitting in this leather so long that my hide's getting raw… hide er… rawhide… pretty good, eh?"

BORDER BADMEN (PRC, 1945): Fuzzy is 32nd cousin to Silas Stockton and goes to the reading of his will. Crooks plan to replace the primary heir with a substitute, so they can get their hands on the Stockton estate. HORSE: Fuzzy rides horse with full blaze.

ANTICS: silly fight with Wally West with Fuzzy butting him in stomach and jaw; gun twirl routine as heavies come through shack door; Fuzzy pushes them for Billy to hit on chin, but when John Cason comes in, he pushes Fuzzy, and Billy hits him instead; licking fingers routine (he usually licks very fast and goes cross-eyed); revolving door in the wall routine with Billy; revolving door-in-the-wall fight scene with Ray Henderson with Fuzzy coming out of the door and kicking him every time he goes round; kicks Budd Buster and Arch Hall.

QUOTES:
1. Fuzzy (failing to get a response from a guard): "Do you think he's dead?"
   Billy: "Or drunk."
   Fuzzy: "Maybe we're both right – he's dead drunk."
2. Bud Osborne (to Fuzzy trying to barge into sheriff's office): "You're staying right here, Whiskers. You're inviting a hole in your gizzard."
3. Fuzzy: "Every time bandits tangle with Fuzzy Q. Jones, they're just digging their own graves."
4. Fuzzy (when he's told price of hotel room): "$20? Listen mister, all we want is a bed. We're not interested in putting a down payment on this barn."
5. Billy (in spooky dark house): "Scout around, and see if you can find an opening."
   Fuzzy: "If I can't find one, I'll build one."

FIGHTING BILL CARSON (PRC, 1945): Allison (I. Stanford Jolley) engineers the Texas legislature into authorizing a bill establishing a bank in Eureka so that he can get all the ranchers' money and savings into one accessible pile for him and his gang. Fuzzy, who owns the general store, is made President of the bank. HORSE: He rides horse with full blaze. If anyone had any doubts about Fuzzy's riding ability, this one has some excellent running-insert close-ups.

ANTICS: slapstick routine in which Fuzzy gets stuck to Bud Osborne and Ray Jones after getting his hands sticky with molasses; rag in back pocket; Fuzzy uses a broom, a roll of paper, and a barrel of apples in silly fight with Kermit Maynard; Fuzzy goes head-first over a counter and a hitching rail; Fuzzy in jail; comic-counting routine – he counts out money for Jimmy Aubrey, but at the same time asks Billy "how many miles?" questions and starts counting from the answer.

QUOTES:
1. Fuzzy: "Outlaws round here are thicker than fleas on a hound dog."
2. Stan Jolley: "Your friend seems to have quite a way with the ladies."
   Fuzzy: "It's the only thing I don't like about Billy Carson – when he's around, women don't pay any attention to me."
3. Fuzzy (to group of townsfolk): "You make more noise than a corral of cows at branding time."
4. Billy (as Fuzzy tries to maneuver a safe into his store): "Heave ho, Fuzz."
   Fuzzy: "If you'd get over here with a little more heave and less ho, I wouldn't mind having you around."
5. Fuzzy: "This money ain't seen the light of day for so long, it's got mildew on it. I bet it'll be glad to get back in circulation."
6. Fuzzy (to Billy): "You couldn't float a loan if it was made out of cork."

PRAIRIE RUSTLERS (PRC, 1945): Billy tangles with his look-a-like cousin Jim Slade who frames him as a cattle rustler. Deputy Sheriff Fuzzy, who also runs the Omaha café, is made sheriff when his superior is murdered.

ANTICS: his legs wobble, and he walks into a post after being punched by Billy Carson's look-a-like cousin; slapstick fight routine with Kermit Maynard – Fuzzy jumps all over him, does a handstand on him on the bar, head butts his stomach until Kermit steps aside and he butts the wall, sprinkles him with pepper so every time Kermit tries to hit him, he sneezes; Billy pulls Fuzzy back by his pants; Fuzzy wins a bicycle in a raffle and everyone scatters as he "learns" to ride it; goes into saloon as Billy knocks Kermit and Bud Osborne out into the street, and Fuzzy is knocked backwards twice into the street as well; sneezes and wipes nose on decorations at a party; he's billed as a "special attraction" at the party to ride the "wild and vicious" bicycle; scratches whiskers; gun twirl; Fuzzy tricks Billy into being sworn in as sheriff by smothering himself in ketchup and pretending he's been shot.

QUOTES:
1. Fuzzy trips over and throws the contents of a tray over a customer who hits him and walks out: "Some folks have no control – fly off the handle too easy."
2. Fuzzy: "I was appointed deputy about the 4th of July in case the boys became too ambunctious."
3. Fuzzy (when Kermit Maynard and Stan Jolley ask for food): "I ain't particular who I wait on."
4. Fuzzy (about the bike): "No two-wheel contraption's gonna get the better of me – I'll make that thing sit up and say uncle." He kicks the bike, and yelps in pain. (To the bike): "If you knew what I was thinking, it would burn the rubber right off them wheels."
5. Fuzzy (to Billy): "You can go paddle your own canoe because if you get into trouble, I ain't gonna help you."
   Billy: "Fuzz, you wouldn't do that to a pal?"
   Fuzzy: "No."
   Billy: "Phew! Scared me there for a minute, boy."
6. Fuzzy (when Billy asks him to tell Karl Hackett that Stan Jolley is a crook): "I feel like an old gasping busybody."
7. Fuzzy: "They made a mistake when they taught women how to talk."

GENTLEMEN WITH GUNS (PRC, 1946): While Fuzzy is waiting for a mail-order bride, McAllister (Steve Darrell) frames him for murder, and then advises Matilda (Patricia Knox) to marry Fuzzy so she will get his ranch and money when he is hung.
HORSE: Fuzzy rides horse with full blaze.
ANTICS: Billy throws two buckets of water on Fuzzy after he burns biscuits, and his house is filled with smoke; fights Steve Darrell with head butts to the stomach and punches to the jaw; another fight with Darrell, pulling his hat down, kicking him in the rear.

QUOTES:
1. Billy (after Fuzzy tells him he's getting married): "Where are you going to find a woman crazy enough to marry an old goat like you?"
2. Fuzzy (about Steve Darrell): "If I had a choice between him and a rattlesnake, I'd take the snake."
3. Fuzzy: "When Matilda sends for me, I'll go through fire and water."
   Billy: "You're liable to get your whiskers singed and your feet wet."
4. Kermit Maynard: "You're supposed to be in jail."
   Fuzzy: "I know, but I'm figuring on getting married, and that's the same as being in jail."
5. Fuzzy: "Where are you going?"
   Matilda: "Home."
   Fuzzy: "You're not going to leave me flat?"
   Matilda: "That's not a bad idea." She knocks Fuzzy flat with a right hand punch.

TERRORS ON HORSEBACK (PRC, 1946): When Fuzzy's niece is killed in a stage holdup, he and Billy go after the killers.
HORSE: Fuzzy rides horse with the full blaze.

ANTICS: Billy orders a sarsaparilla for Fuzzy, but he spits it out – he calls it a "belly wash"; gun twirl; Lane Bradford and Al Ferguson both call Fuzzy "half pint";

QUOTES:
1. Billy: "He's hot-headed, and flies off the handle, but Fuzzy wouldn't hurt a fly if he wasn't driven to it. They just don't come any better than old Fuzz."
2. Billy: "Fuzzy, just keep your mouth closed."
   Fuzzy: "But there's something funny going on."
   Billy: "Shut up."

3. Fuzzy: "I ain't putting my guns down until the whole bunch of you bone-picking coyotes are brought to justice."
   Bud Osborne: "Listen to the whiskers run."
4. Fuzzy: "I'm considered the best cook in Lincoln County – I'll whip you up a meal that will make your belly sing."
   Osborne: "Untie the runt, and let's see what he can do."
5. Fuzzy: "There's one thing sure, I ain't letting no gun-slinging range tramps take me prisoner." Lane Bradford: "All right, reach you hombres."
   Fuzzy (shoots hands in the air): "Yes sir."
6. Fuzzy (dropping a stick of dynamite into the stove): "You're gonna get a bang out of this meal."

GHOST OF HIDDEN VALLEY (PRC, 1946): Dawson (Charlie King) is running rustled cattle across the abandoned Trenton (John Meredith) ranch which has a reputation of being haunted. This normally keeps people away, but then an heir arrives from England. HORSE: Fuzzy rides horse with full blaze.

ANTICS: Fuzzy puts on sissy pose in an impression of the dude from Oxford, England; silly fight with John Cason; sits up, gives silly grin, goes cross-eyed and falls back; Billy's horse Falcon's head swings round and strikes Fuzzy a blow on the shoulder; coat- on, coat-off slapstick routine with Jimmy Aubrey.

QUOTES:
1. Fuzzy (trying to figure out what to do next): "Now, if I was a ghost."
   Billy: "You will be if you don't shut up and go to sleep. I'll see to it personally."
2. Fuzzy: "It could have been rustlers who have been haunting the valley."
   Billy: "You're beginning to show signs of intelligence."
3. Fuzzy: "Hey, why didn't you wait until I got back? You know I enjoy a good fight."
   Billy: "Sorry, Fuzzy, but our friend wanted immediate service."
   Fuzzy (looks at a battered Charles King): "Looks like he got it."

PRAIRIE BADMEN (PRC, 1946): Medicine-show owner Doc Lattimer (Ed Cassidy) has a map leading to a cache of stolen gold. The Doc wants to see the money returned, but his son and a gang of crooks think otherwise. HORSE: Fuzzy rides horse with full blaze.

ANTICS: falls off show wagon when Charles King and his gang tow it away; Fuzzy's war-dance routine after mistakenly drinking turpentine instead of elixir; Fuzzy keeps his watch in his boot; he swings back a rock to throw at outlaws, but knocks Billy out instead; silly fight with Kermit Maynard, tickling him with feathers, etc; calls Billy a "hoodoo" when he gets sacked from medicine show; Billy pulls Fuzzy back by the pants; drunk act; gun twirl; burned by campfire; he puts his boot on his head and foot in his hat; leaning gag; head-over-heels through shack door.

QUOTES:
1. Fuzzy is a medicine-show spieler dressed in full-length, Indian-head dress: "Lay your dollar on the line – then go home and make your wife think she's got a new husband… and for you lady folks vice versa."
2. Billy (when he gets attention from Patricia Knox): "You wouldn't happen to be jealous, you old goat?"
3. Billy (to Fuzzy): "Will you stop snoring?"
   Fuzzy (wakes up): "I'm sure I heard a horse coming this way."
   Billy: "A nightmare."
4. Billy (after a rock hits Fuzzy): "Your head sounds as hollow as a pumpkin."
5. Billy: "It would ruin Fuzzy to have money – couldn't get a hat to fit him."
6. Patricia Knox: "Billy Carson, you're a very nice person.
   Billy: "I bet you say that to all the boys."
   Fuzzy: "She ain't never said it to me, yet." Patricia (kisses him): "Fuzzy, you're a dear." Fuzzy falls over and, is dragged away by Billy.
7. Fuzzy (to Billy): "Why don't you do me a favor and play dead?"

OVERLAND RIDERS (PRC, 1946): Billy buys Barkley's (Slim Whitaker) cattle, but Landreau (Jack O'Shea) kills Barkley in a scheme to grab his ranch. Fuzzy rides horse with full blaze. Grey hairs starting to appear in whiskers.

ANTICS: smokes cigar; strikes match on his beard; blows smoke over Patti McCarty in stagecoach, making her cough; he leans out of window to shoot at chasing outlaws, but almost falls out, and has to be hauled back by Patti; kicks Al Ferguson in the

Jack Rockwell is the sheriff once again.

It appears Fuzzy and Budd Buster are seeing things eye to eye.

"No problem, Lash. I can taste the message."

"I'll take the front, and you go around back, Fuzzy."

rear to get him moving; Patti hits Fuzzy with stagecoach door; Fuzzy trips over sidewalk; funny dismount; rag in back pocket; strikes match on trousers to light a cigar; Charles Whitaker slams door in his face; shuts himself in an empty cell and then yells: "Let me outta here!"

QUOTES:
1. Fuzzy (when Patti McCarty shows concern for Billy's gunshot wound): "He probably jumped over sideways to get hisself creased with a bullet."
2. Fuzzy: "I don't like outlaws – I like to see them strung higher than a kite."
3. Black Jack O'Shea (when Fuzzy says he wants to buy a piece of land to farm, settle down and get married): "We'll see he gets a piece of land – six-foot by six-foot."
4. Fuzzy (to Billy): "You've laughed at me every time I've had ambitions to be important."

OUTLAWS OF THE PLAINS (PRC, 1946): Fuzzy is "advised" by an Indian-spirit guide who gets him to persuade folk in Showdown Flats to buy worthless property. HORSE: Fuzzy ride horse with full blaze.

ANTICS: rag in back pocket; wobbly legs; it's Fuzzy, rather than Billy, who chases after King at the finish, and bulldogs him.

QUOTES:
1. Charles King: "Say, Fuzzy, maybe that Indian pal of yours could tell you where to dig a little gold dust on this claim."
   Fuzzy: "Ain't you found nothin' yet?"
   King: "Not enough to fill a gnat's tooth."
2. King: "You bandy-legged little scarecrow – I should fill you so full of bullets, they could work you as a gold mine."
3. King (to Fuzzy): "I ain't killed a guy for over a week, and I wouldn't trust you with myself."
4. Townsman Jack Henderson: "Oh, Mr. Jones, when would be a good time to sell my crops?" Fuzzy: "Oh, about the first."
   Henderson: "The first of what?"
   Fuzzy: "The first chance you get!"
5. Fuzzy (to his "spirit guide"): "Standing Pine! I gotta couple of things I want to tell you." (When he doesn't get a response) "I wonder if he belongs to the union."
6. Fuzzy: "Hey, wait a minute boys – don't crowd me! I'm formin' a big organization, and you're all welcome as soon as things get ripe."
   John Cason: "Yeah, and when it is, we'll be on hand to pick the plum."
   Black Jack O'Shea: "Provided Billy Carson doesn't upset the apple cart."
7. Billy: "Well, you can include me out. I haven't got $50,000 to be buying gold mines from crazy people."
8. Fuzzy: "Standing Pine told me where I could find this big claim."
   Billy: "Who's Standing Pine?"
   Fuzzy: He's my Indian guide. He's a spirit.
   Billy: "A spirit? Fuzz, you better keep that cork in the bottle. Those spirits are going to get you in trouble."
   Fuzzy: "Oh well, they laughed at Columbus, too."
9. Billy: "I'm going, Fuzz. When that lynching party gets ready to singe your whiskers, you can call for me."

LAW OF THE LASH (PRC, 1947): Chancing on a stagecoach holdup, United States Marshal Cheyenne Davis finds clues that help him rid a town of murdering gunslingers. Fuzzy rides horse with full blaze.

ANTICS: Fuzzy threads a needle and goes cross-eyed; rag in back pocket; he sends a message by putting two broken telegraph lines together, claiming that if he puts the wire in his mouth, he can "taste" the answer. When he does, he gets an electric shock and falls over; plays checkers; leaning gag.

QUOTES:
1. Fuzzy: "Hey, here's an empty sack, and here's a list of what to put in it."
   Lash: "Fuzzy, your list is just like a letter; it always starts out the same."
   Fuzzy: "Oh, you mean a sort of Dear Sir?"
   Lash: "No – six plugs of chewin' tobacco."
   Fuzzy: "Well, I gotta have some kind of stimulant."
   Lash: "You old buzzard, if those hills come through with what I think they will, we'll both have all the stimulant we want, and it won't be tobacco."
2. Fuzzy: "Well, Mister, throwin' away my ginger beer is right wasteful of my invigoration."
   Black Jack O'Shea: "And you're wasteful of conversation. From now on, get to the point."

BORDER FEUD (PRC, 1947): Crook stirs up a feud between two families who have a joint interest in a valuable mine. Fuzzy is sheriff of Red Gulch. HORSE: rides horse with full blaze.

ANTICS: The second time Fuzzy is punched, when he tries to break up a brawl he laughs, goes cross-eyed, and slumps to the floor; he spits; gun twirl; burns his rear on a stove when he is pushed by Bob Duncan; tries to use bullwhip, but ends up wrapped in it; whips lump of wood, pulls it forward and it hits him on the head, and he does a forward flip; catches fingers in a knothole.

QUOTES:
1. Sheriff Ed Cassidy: "Fuzzy Jones? That name is familiar."
   Lash: "I'm sure a lot of folks have heard about Fuzzy. He's a funny old codger – usually manages to do the wrong thing at the right time. But he's a good lawman in spite of all the confusion."
2. Fuzzy (after putting members of feuding families in separate cells): "Keepin' you two roosters separated oughta mean the feud will die a natural death... that is, unless looks can kill."
3. Fuzzy (to Lash): "Well, I don't get it. Me a sheriff and you a marshal, and we're both fugitives."
4. Bob Duncan (on seeing Fuzzy whack his thumb as he puts up a warning sign for the feuding families): "I figured you'd wind up a casualty in that feud sooner or later."

PIONEER JUSTICE (PRC, 1947): Three United States marshals are murdered by crooks involved in a massive land grab to drive out ranchers around Barton City and the Waterhole ghost town. HORSE: Fuzzy rides horse with full blaze.

ANTICS: one-handed cigarette-making routine; gun twirl; alarm clock routine – Fuzzy ends up shooting the clock; He ends the movie as sheriff.

QUOTES:
1. Fuzzy (when Lash asks for witnesses to small rancher's murder, no one speaks up): "All deaf, dumb, and blind."
2. Fuzzy: "If it ain't one thing it's another – I'm gonna get me a new partner."
   Lash: "Okay, so long."
   Fuzzy: "What's the matter – you trying to get rid of me?"

GHOST TOWN RENEGADES (PRC, 1947): Honest landowners are killed and new deeds for their land are forged by crooks after the gold. HORSE: Fuzzy rides horse with full blaze. Much stock footage is lifted from the first three films in the series.

ANTICS: Fuzzy has a 'watchamacallit' for locating treasures and veins of ore; silly fight with Terry Frost in which he head butts him in stomach and then head butts wall – he also kicks Lane Bradford in the face; kicks his hat up and puts it on his head; funny fight with Jack Ingram; moving-hat routine similar to "Mysterious Rider" but with a gopher instead of a cat; routine in which he looks in a mirror, and is frightened by himself; sticky-paper routine.

QUOTES:
1. Fuzzy: "You know I don't believe in those stories about spooks, but I'm still scared of them."
2. Lash (when a desktop springs up and hits Fuzzy, revealing a vital clue): "Looks like you've hit the jackpot."
   Fuzzy: "You mean the jackpot hit me."

STAGE TO MESA CITY (PRC, 1947): Supposedly paralyzed, postmaster Padgett (George Chesebro) is the man behind the attempts to put the Watson (Brad Slaven) stage line out of business. Fuzzy is a deputy marshal, and rides horse with full blaze.

ANTICS: Fuzzy has a metal Sitting Bull talisman for luck – it saves his life when a bullet hits it; he is hit, and goes head over heels; goes over the back of a chair; Fuzzy is left as sheriff at the finish.

QUOTES:
1. Fuzzy: "Every time we investigate something, bullets start flying like hailstones."
2. Fuzzy (when Lash rounds up Marshall Reed): "So you got the lawyer? Let's make a corpus delectable or something out of him."

RETURN OF THE LASH (PRC, 1947): Crooks want the Grant (Brad Slaven) ranch because of its water supply, and the fact the railroad is coming through it. HORSE: Fuzzy rides horse with full blaze.

ANTICS: Dee Cooper throws Fuzzy through a window; Roy Butler calls Fuzzy "mattress face"; gun twirl; Fuzzy gets in a fight, and ends up with a box on his head and with his hand caught in a can; hit over the head with a chair; wobbly legs; rag in back pocket; pulls himself up by the seat of his pants to mount a horse; he has a bag of tools that opens a jail door, bureau, and safe; comic safe-opening routine.

QUOTES:
1. Fuzzy: "There ain't a man living faster on the draw than I am."
2. Fuzzy (to Lane Bradford): "Get out before my finger slips (off the trigger)."
3. Fuzzy (after he loses his memory): "I might not like my old self when I get to know me."

THE FIGHTING VIGILANTES (PRC, 1947): Crooks, who wreck food-supply trains so they can keep their own prices sky-high, are attacked by vigilantes. HORSE: Fuzzy rides horse with full blaze.

ANTICS: Fuzzy writes poetry – Lash calls him "my poetic sidekick"; Fuzzy leans on wagon wheel, and the wagon collapses; kicks Carl Mathews in the rear; walks into a wall; single-handed cigarette-rolling routine; spits across room to put a light out; lights match on his jeans; at the finish, Fuzzy recites a poem at the top of a ladder, Lash whips the ladder away, and Fuzzy hits the ground with his head through a sign.

QUOTES:
1. Fuzzy: (to Lash): "Every time you see a girl, I smell trouble."
2. Lash: "My marshal's badge is our ace in the hole, so keep it under your hat."
   Fuzzy: "I ain't got room – I've got plenty under there now."
3. Fuzzy: "Take it easy – they're not water pistols they're toting."

CHEYENNE TAKES OVER (PRC, 1947): It turns into a working holiday for Lash when he arrives at a ranch for a break, and discovers the owner has been murdered and replaced by an impostor. HORSE: Fuzzy rides horse with full blaze.

ANTICS: Fuzzy is knocked down by stray punches as Lash battles John Merton and Brad Slaven; Fuzzy falls to the ground when the spade he's leaning on is kicked away by Merton; he falls asleep on a hitching rail; Merton refers to Fuzzy as Lash's "goat-faced friend"; Fuzzy loses a tooth in a silly fight with Merton; gun twirl; kicks George Chesebro in the face.

QUOTES:
1. Fuzzy: "Cross my heart and hope to swallow a pitchfork."
2. Fuzzy: "I'm the toughest man the marshal's office has got working for them. Besides, I'm the best rider they got (mounts his horse and ends up facing the tail) Hey, who turned my horse around?"

DEAD MAN'S GOLD (Western Adventure/Screen Guild, 1948): When crooks murder a man for his gold, Lash sets out to track down the mystery head of the gang. Fuzzy rides horse with full blaze.

ANTICS: When Lash whips a glass out of a crook's hand, Fuzzy tells him he's slipping because a few drops of drink were spilled; when Fuzzy's nose itches it means "trouble is just round the corner"; John Cason calls Fuzzy a "funny-looking straw mutt"; Fuzzy kicks Cason in the rear; Fuzzy runs and trips over, firing his gun; the leaning gag; gun twirl; when Peggy kisses Fuzzy at the fade-out (in a speeded up sequence), he yells "whoopee," jumps on his horse and rides off.

QUOTES:
1. Fuzzy: "My tongue is so dry; if I blew my breath, I'd blow up a dust storm."
2. Fuzzy (to Peggy Stewart: "You tell that jug-headed foreman of yours to tend to his own business, or I'm gonna cloud up and snow all over him."

MARK OF THE LASH (Western Adventure/Screen Guild, 1948): Red Rock's self-appointed sheriff (Harry Cody) closes off the local ranchers' water supply and murders (by mistake) the man he believes has been sent to investigate the matter. HORSE: Fuzzy rides a horse with a full blaze, but it's not the regular one.

ANTICS: Fuzzy tells his Buffalo Bill stories to townsfolk who all walk away and leave him talking to himself; he tries his singled-handed cigarette-rolling routine, and looks out at the audience (Oliver Hardy style) when it doesn't work; goes cross-eyed, and licks his fingers; he's jostled by John Cason and his milk goes all over him; Cason takes a swing at Lash, and hits Fuzzy instead, knocking him for a loop; Fuzzy's foot gets stuck in a spittoon – he kicks Ray Jones in the face as he gets spittoon off; scratches whiskers; gun twirl; slips off the back of his horse; Fuzzy sets a trap for prowlers, but steps in it himself, and ends up hanging upside down from a tree.

QUOTES:
1. Fuzzy: "When I used to ride with Buffalo Bill, he could sniff a buffalo from 10 miles away."
2. Fuzzy (shoots Lee Roberts' gun out of his hand): "Little boys who play with fire are liable to get hurt."
3. Fuzzy: "I was so hungry I ate a whole ham before Buffalo Bill told me it was the hind leg of a buffalo."
4. Fuzzy: "I remember one time, when I was riding with Buffalo Bill, I met a fella who left his wife in Kansas City, went to California looking for gold, and one day he set off a charge of dynamite that blew him all the way back to Kansas City in his own backyard."
5. Fuzzy (to Lash): "I'll be so close to you it will look like there's only one of us".

FRONTIER REVENGE (1948): United States Marshals (Lash and Fuzzy) pose as the Dawson Brothers to get the goods on the outlaw gang led by outwardly respectable citizen Rago (Ray Bennett). HORSE: Fuzzy rides a paint horse.

ANTICS: Fuzzy catches gun when Lash whips it out of crook's hand; kicks Jim Bannon in the rear; gun twirl; walks into wall; flicks tongue to lick pencil.

QUOTE: Fuzzy (to Jim Bannon): "If you wanna live to a ripe old age never ask a man what part of the country he comes from; it's liable to give you poisoning – lead poisoning."

OUTLAW COUNTRY (Western Adventure/Screen Guild, 1949): Lash and Fuzzy are sent south of the border to break up a counterfeiting gang, and meet up with Lash's twin brother, the Frontier Phantom. HORSE: Fuzzy rides a paint horse.

ANTICS: Fuzzy reads book how to hypnotize people and become a wizard; funny sneeze; Fuzzy hypnotizes Bob Terhune by saying Alakazam, but is knocked for a loop when he says Alakazim and breaks the spell; Fuzzy kicks Lee Roberts in the rear; Steve Dunhill calls Fuzzy a "crazy old goat"; Fuzzy slips on some soap.

QUOTES:
1. Fuzzy: "One day when I'm Fuzzy the Wuzard… I mean wizard... you won't have so much to laugh about."
2. Fuzzy: "I once bet a plugged nickel on a weasel race."

SON OF BILLY THE KID (Western Adventure/Screen Guild, 1949): Twenty years after Billy the Kid's death, United States Marshal Jack Garrett (Lash LaRue) rides into Baldwin City, where Billy is living under an assumed name as a banker. Fuzzy is a stage driver, porter, ticket agent, and sheriff in Baldwin City and does not know Jack Garrett at the start of the movie. Horse: Fuzzy rides a paint horse.

ANTICS: Fuzzy's trying to keep his eyes-open routine; rag in back pocket; Fuzzy gets stuck between two rocks; fadeout with June Carr giving Fuzzy a piggy-back ride with wedding music playing.

QUOTES:
1. June Carr: "Don't you have any chivalry?"
   Fuzzy: "No, but I have a lot of trouble with this knee here sometimes."
2. Fuzzy: "Jumping Jehoshaphat and Kansas City tadpoles – it's the bank!"
3. Fuzzy to June Carr: "What are you thinking?"
   June: "What do you think I'm thinking?"
   Fuzzy: "If you're thinking what I think you're thinking, and I think what you think you're thinking, you've got another think coming."
4. Fuzzy (asked to describe one of the outlaw gang): "He's a short, tall, slim, heavy-set fella – come to think of it, I don't know."
5. Fuzzy (referring to June Carr): "I'm in trouble with this she-male."

6. June: "This fugitive from a barbershop proposed to me."
   Fuzzy: "All I said was, she's got a hide like a porcupine in the moonlight."
   June: "That's getting romantic where I come from."
   Fuzzy: "Feet … do your duty."

SON OF A BADMAN (Western Adventure/Screen Guild, 1949): Lash and Fuzzy are United States Marshals on the trail of El Sombre and his gang in Star City, and discover the sheriff is in cahoots with the outlaws. HORSE: Fuzzy rides a paint horse.

ANTICS: Fuzzy gets a toothache every time there's going to be trouble; Fuzzy lassos Jack Ingram who rides off, and pulls Fuzzy along in the sitting position; pulled back by seat of pants by Lash; Lash gets Fuzzy out of a deep sleep by saying "Let's eat."; Zon Murray calls Fuzzy an "old codger"; gun twirl; runs into a wall; runs into a hitching rail; Fuzzy falls backward against a wall in surprise when a Piute Indian (Frank Lackteen) speaks perfect English – a chief's headdress falls off the wall on to Fuzzy, and he says "How."

QUOTES:
1. Fuzzy doesn't want to go to the dentist: "After (the tooth) is out, how are we going to know if we are in trouble?"
2. Fuzzy (in the dentist's office): "I'm going outside – I forgot something."
   Lash: "What did you forget?" Fuzzy: "To stay there."
3. Dentist (Michael Whalen): "I'm gonna make a new man outta you."
   Fuzzy: "Don't worry about making a new man out of me.. I want my friends to recognize me."
4. Fuzzy (jumps when he sees himself in a mirror): "Hey, Lash, I've got the ugliest looking hombre cornered here you ever saw."

THE DALTONS' WOMEN (1950): The Dalton Gang has moved west, and taken on new identities and Lash and Fuzzy are on their trail helped by a female Pinkerton agent. HORSE: Fuzzy rides paint horse.

ANTICS: when Lash whips Terry Frost's gun out of his hand Fuzzy catches it; Fuzzy runs into a post; his itchy palm makes him feel lucky; flicks pack of cards in sheriff's face to enable escape; single-handed cigarette roll routine; rag in back pocket; gun twirl; Pamela Blake kisses him and he goes cross-eyed and falls flat on his face.

QUOTES:
1. Fuzzy: "Bartender, fix me up with a schooner of milk."
   Bartender (Cliff Taylor): "Milk? You'll want a little sting in it, of course?"
   Fuzzy: "No, I've got sting enough in me already."
2. Fuzzy: "I've been prospecting."
   Terry Frost: "Any good?"
   Fuzzy: "Pretty good… outside of the gold bug."
   Frost: "Gold bug?"
   Fuzzy: "Ain't you never heard of the gold bug… it's sorta like a termite only they eat nothing but gold… ate me out of two years hard work (Frost grabs him) "Hey, wait a minute, that's a joke, son."

KING OF THE BULLWHIP (Western Adventure/Screen Guild, 1951): Marshals Lash and Fuzzy are on the trail of whip-slinging, masked robber El Azote. When Lash impersonates El Azote, it brings the bandit out into the open. HORSE: Fuzzy rides a paint horse.

ANTICS: Fuzzy uses a catapult on Lewis's gang after they rob a bank

QUOTES:
1. George Lewis: "Haven't I seen you somewhere before, Whiskers?" Fuzzy: "Mebbe." Lewis: "You look like someone I know." Michael Whalen: "Been here long?" Fuzzy: "Mebbe." Lewis: "Is that the only word you know?" Fuzzy: "Mebbe." Lewis (grabs him): "Look when I'm talking to you, I want answers. Are you going to answer my questions?" Fuzzy: "Mebbe." Lewis (pulls a gun): "Does this make a difference?" Fuzzy starts to say "maybe," but changes it to "Uh-huh." Lewis calls him "mopface."
2. Lash: "Shall we walk, Mr. Jones?"
   Fuzzy: "I don't mind if we do, Mr. LaRue."

3. Lewis: "I am very sorry, but I just came over to invite you two boys to a party that's waiting." Fuzzy: "What kind?" Lewis: "A hanging party."
4. Fuzzy (threatened with hanging by Lewis and his gang): "You can't do this to me; I've got important friends. Why, there's Wyatt Earp, Wild Bill Hickok, and Kit Carson… they'll come down here and avenge me."
5. Fuzzy: "I'm a personal friend of Wild Bill, Pawnee Bill, and Buffalo Bill."
6. Tom Neal: "I don't know whether to hire your friend – he's pretty old for this type of thing." Fuzzy: "Old? What do you mean old? Why I was riding with Billy the Kid…."
7. Fuzzy (to Lash, getting confused between him and El Azote): "Hey, for a minute, I thought you was him, but he's he and you're you, so you can't be him"
8. Fuzzy (to Roy Butler): "Sure I knew them all… why I ate beans out of the same can with Billy the Kid, walked with Wyatt Earp over in Tombstone; old Doc Holliday pulled a tooth out right about in here and Belle Starr – she wanted to marry me, but I was a little bit young at the time."
Butler: "You really knew all of them?"
Fuzzy: "I used to hunt with Buffalo Bill ... outshot him three to one."
Butler: "Him, too? You're not spoofing me are you, Fuzzy?"
Fuzzy: "Did I know Buffalo Bill? Me and him were blood brothers adopted by the same Indian tribe. If I'm lying to you, I hope my knees buckle right in the middle and I go to sleep for two months."
Lash walks in with Buffalo Bill (Tex Cooper), and introduces him to Fuzzy: "I'd like you to meet an old friend of yours, Buffalo Bill."
Fuzzy: "B..B..Buffalo Bill?" His legs wobble and he lies down, and goes to sleep.

THE THUNDERING TRAIL (Western Adventure, 1951): Marshals Lash and Fuzzy are assigned to escort the new Governor to Capitol City, but an outlaw gang goes all out to stop them. The last reel or so lifted intact from SON OF BILLY THE KID. Horse: Fuzzy rides a paint horse.

ANTICS: Fuzzy's nose itches when there's trouble.

QUOTES:
1. Fuzzy (to Bud Osborne): "I've got a weak heart, and too much excitement might do me in."
2. Fuzzy: "Don't make any moves because my trigger finger's getting itchier than my nose."
3. Fuzzy (to John Cason): "Take this mangy coyote with you before I skin him alive and use his hide for a rug."
4. Fuzzy goofs and calls Archie Twitchell Judge, but cameras keep rolling, and Fuzzy corrects himself: "Pardon me, I mean Governor."

THE VANISHING OUTPOST (Western Adventure, 1951): Lash and Fuzzy help a Pinkerton agent to bring to justice a gang of train robbers who use coded messages in their outlawry. There's lots of stock footage from at least four earlier LaRue movies. HORSE: Fuzzy rides a paint horse.

ANTICS: Fuzzy is bothered by toothache which allows footage from SON OF A BADMAN.

QUOTES:
1. Lash: "This town looks dead."
   Fuzzy: "Don't use that word – it gives me the hoobie jeebies."
2. Fuzzy (to Lash): "I'll be so close to you it will look like there's only one of us."
3. Fuzzy: "Just because you're smarter than me doesn't mean I'm dumber than you."
4. Fuzzy: (talking about the dentists): "I'm not going to one of those chipper choppers." Then as he walks out of the saloon, someone walks in, and the swinging door knocks his aching tooth out."

THE BLACK LASH (Western Adventure, 1952): Lash put Deuce Rago in jail, but now he's out, and he and his gang are into silver hi-jacking. This is a sequel to FRONTIER REVENGE with lots of stock footage. Fuzzy mentions the Frontier Phantom at the start, which results in even more stock footage. HORSE: Fuzzy rides a paint horse.

ANTICS: gun twirl; Fuzzy pokes his tongue out at Lash after he cuts in when Peggy Stewart is sweet-talking Fuzzy, and takes her to jail.

QUOTES:
1. Clarke Stevens: "I'll sue you for everything you've got." Fuzzy: "You won't get much; I'm wearing everything I got."
2. Fuzzy (to Stevens): "If you don't stay until he (Lash) gets here, I'm gonna step right on your corns."
3. Fuzzy (after being elected sheriff): "When the cowboys find out that Fuzzy Q. Jones is sheriff, there ain't gonna be no more shooting. Everything's gonna be peaceful and quiet." This cues bunch of cowboys riding into town for a Saturday-night shoot-em-up.

THE FRONTIER PHANTOM (Western Adventure, 1952): Lash is arrested on suspicion of being The Frontier Phantom. Lash tells the sheriff the story of the Phantom who is his twin brother in order to clear his name. HORSE: Fuzzy rides a paint horse.

ANTICS: Fuzzy sniffs sarsaparilla, and makes a face and holds his nose while he drinks it. Then he twists his ear, and spits it out; gun twirl.

QUOTES:
1. Bud Osborne: "Bat an eyelash, and I'll touch off this cannon."
   Fuzzy: "Lash, don't breathe – them's double-barreled shotguns. I don't mind being pickled, but I don't like to be peppered."
2. Clarke Stevens: "If you and Frontier aren't the same fella, I'll eat my hat."
   Fuzzy: "You'd better get some cream and sugar because it's going to be a little rough going down."
3. Sheriff Archie Twitchell: "That's the Frontier Phantom, or I'll eat my hat."
   Fuzzy: "Some folks will eat anything around here."
4. Lash: "If Mantell rides into town, and you're in bed asleep, they'll laugh you out of office in a week."
   Twitchell: "If Mantell comes here, I'll get him."
5. Fuzzy: "Sleepwalking, or just riding a nightmare?"
6. Fuzzy: "How about those sandwiches and coffee?"
   Stevens: "It's on its way over."
   Fuzzy: "That's how I like my coffee when it's strong enough to walk over here by itself."
7. Fuzzy: "Those dirty crooks forced me into a gambling game, which is against my principles."
8. Fuzzy (to Virginia Herrick): "Keep that beanery open – I'll be over in 15 minutes.
   Herrick: "Sure, come on over. My husband's the cook. He makes terrific hash. Might even make hash out of you."

PHOTO GALLERY

Fuzzy casts a spell on stuntman, Bob Terhune (son of Max Terhune).

"Who turned my horse around?"

"Hey, Blackie, how many fingers do you see?"

Fuzzy in his new longhandles.

Buster, Glenn Strange, and Fuzzy.

Bob Brooks (Fuzzy Q. Jones) Look-A-Like

Fuzzy and his cure-all elixer.

"Ready to see my one-handed roll?"

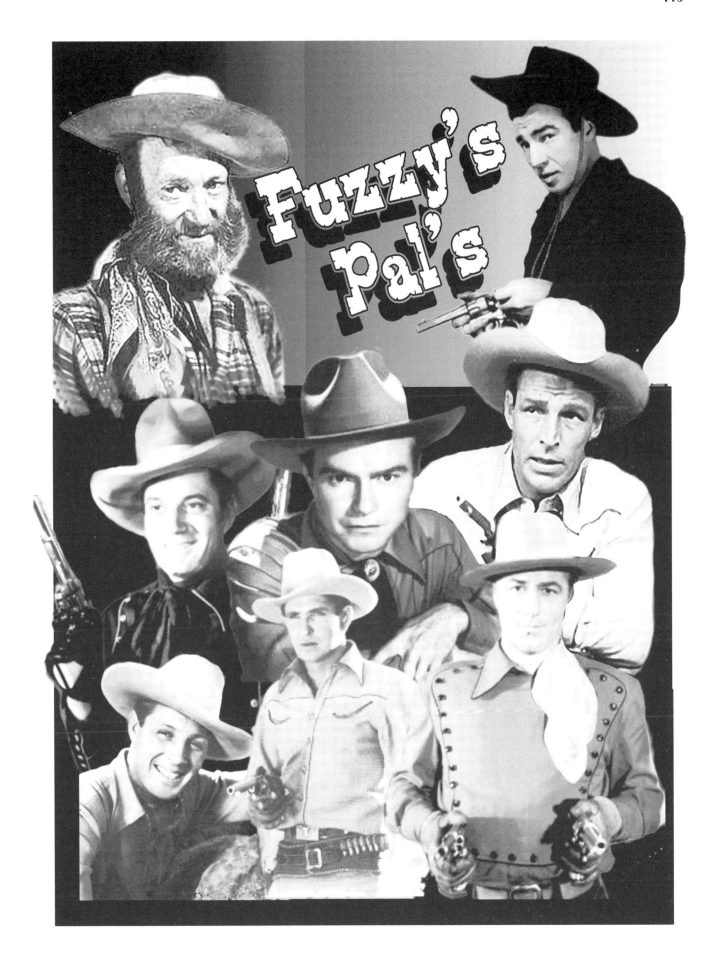

"Can I help it because I'm so handsome?"

Fuzzy, Lash, and Jennifer Holt.

Peggy Stewart, Lash, and Fuzzy.

Buster Crabbe, Glenn Strange, and Fuzzy.

Fuzzy and Lash look down John Merton's Rifle barrel.

Budd Buster, Buster and Fuzzy get the drop on Stan Jolley and Steve Darrell.

Lois January and Fred Scott admire White Dust.

Fuzzy, George J. Lewis and Lash in a scene from KING OF THE BULLWHIP (Western Adventure, 1950).

"That's all, folks."

ABOUT THE AUTHOR

Reared in Oak Ridge, Tennessee, Bobby Copeland began going to the Saturday matinee B-Western movies at nearby theaters. He was immediately impressed by the moral code of these films, and has tried to pattern his life after the example set by the cowboy heroes. After graduating from high school and attending Carson-Newman College and the University of Tennessee, he set out to raise a family and start a career at the Oak Ridge National Laboratory. His love for the old Western films was put on the shelf and lay dormant for some 35 years. One Saturday, in the 1980s, he happened to turn on his television, and the station was showing a Lash LaRue picture. This rekindled his interest. He contacted the TV program's host ("Marshal" Andy Smalls), and was invited to appear on the program. Since that time, Bobby has had some 150 articles published, contributed to over 15 books, made several speeches, appeared on television over 50 times, and has been interviewed by several newspapers and four independent radio stations as well as the Public Radio Broadcasting System to provide commentary and promote interest in B-Western films. In 1985, he was a co-founder of the Knoxville, Tennessee-based "Riders of the Silver Screen Club," serving five times as president. He initiated and edited the club's newsletter. In 1996, his book Trail Talk was published by Empire Publishing, Inc. (one of the world's largest publishers of books on Western films and performers). Since then, he has authored 16 other B-Western books. In 2002, Bobby was a featured speaker at the Tennessee Mountain Writers' Conference.

He has attended some 65 Western film festivals, and met many of the Western movie performers. He continues to contribute articles to the various Western magazines, and he is a regular columnist for Western Clippings. In 1988, Bobby received the "Buck Jones Rangers Trophy," presented annually to individuals demonstrating consistent dedication to keeping the spirit of the B-Western alive. In 1994, Don Key (Empire Publishing) and Boyd Magers (Video West, Inc. & Western Clippings) awarded Bobby the "Buck Rainey Shoot-em-Ups Pioneer Award," which yearly honors a fan who has made significant contributions towards the preservation of interest in the B-Westerns. In 2006, he received the "Saddle Pal Award" from The Old Cowboy Picture Show magazine and in 2007 the "Edward A. Wall Award" from the Williamsburg Film Festival.

Bobby is an active member of Central Baptist Church in Oak Ridge, Tennessee. He retired in 1996 after 40 years at the same workplace. His plans are to continue with his church work, write more B-Western articles, and enjoy his retirement with his faithful sidekick Joan.

SELECTED BIBLIOGRAPHIES

Adams, Les and Rainey, Buck, *Shoot-Em-Ups*
Anderson, Chuck, The Old Corral website
Copeland, Bobby J., *Trail Talk*
Copeland, Bobby J., *B-Western Boot Hill*
International Movie Database
McCord, Merrill T., *Brothers of the West*
Miller, Don, *Hollywood Corral*
Rothel, David, *Those Great Cowboy Sidekicks*
Rothel, David, *Lash LaRue – King of the Bullwhip*
Kark Whitezel, *Buster Crabbe: A Self-Portrait*

INDIVIDUALS

Jerry Baumann
R.T. Blackwood
Gene Blottner
John Brooker
Buddy Bryant
Don Calhoun
Joe Copeland
Paul Dellinger
Ronnie Glass
Jim Hamby
Bruce Hickey

Larry Hopper
Clyde Lester
Colin Momber
Ross Pitt
Jim Vecchio
Billy Weathersby
Grady Franklin
Jimmy Glover
Tommy Scott
Barney Miller
Bob Brooks

B-WESTERN BOOT HILL

A Final Tribute to the Cowboys and Cowgirls Who Rode the Saturday Matinee Movie Range

by Bobby J. Copeland

$15.00 (+ $3.00 s/h)

NEWLY REVISED AND UPDATED! Now includes the obituaries of Rex Allen, Dale Evans, Walter Reed, Clayton Moore, and others. *You asked for it—now here it is . . . an extensively updated version of B-WESTERN BOOT HILL. (The first printing sold out!) An easy reference guide with hundreds of new entries, updates, and revisions. If you've worn out your original BOOT HILL, or are looking for a more complete B-Western reference book, this is the book for you!*

* 1000+ ENTRIES *
The Most Complete List Ever Assembled of Birth Dates, Death Dates, and Real Names of Those Beloved B-Western Performers.

* IT'S A LITERARY MILESTONE *
Bobby Copeland has produced a literary milestone which surely will rank at the top among those important Western film history books printed within the past 30 years. *Richard B. Smith, III*

* OBITUARIES AND BURIAL LOCATIONS *
Through the years, Bobby Copeland has collected actual obituaries of hundreds of B-Western heroes, heavies, helpers, heroines and sidekicks. Also included is a listing of actual burial locations of many of the stars.

ROY BARCROFT: King of the Badmen
by Bobby J. Copeland

A WONDERFUL BOOK ABOUT A GREAT CHARACTER ACTOR

In this book, you will find:
- A detailed biography
- Foreword by Monte Hale
- How he selected the name "Roy Barcroft"
- Letters and comments by Roy
- Roy's views about his co-workers
- Co-workers' comments about Roy
- Roy's fans speak out
- Other writers' opinions of Roy Barcraft
- Filmography

$15.00 (+ $3.00 s/h)

CHARLIE KING

We called him "Blackie"
by Bobby J. Copeland

Who was the "baddest" of the badmen?
Many will say it was Charlie King.

This book is a salute to Charles "Blackie" King— one of the premiere B-Western badmen.

Includes:
- The most comprehensive information ever printed on "Blackie"
- The truth about Charlie's death... including his death certificate
- Comments by noted Western film historians
- Remarks by co-workers
- Writers' opinions of Charlie's acting and his career
- Cowboys with whom he worked
- Studios that employed him
- Filmography

$15.00 (+ $3.00 s/h)

EMPIRE PUBLISHING, INC. • 3130 US HIGHWAY 220 • MADISON, NC 27025 • PHONE 336-427-5850 • FAX 336-427-7372

GABBY HAYES
King of the Cowboy Comics

Finally, a long overdue book on one of B-Westerns' greatest sidekicks and character actors.

Includes:

Gabby's Biography
His films with Hoppy, Wild Bill, Roy and others.
Gabby on radio and TV
His comic books
His Boys Ranch
Popularity rankings
Gabbyisms
Merchandising Gabby
His Westerns in review
His life after his screen career
Remarks by his fans and co-workers
Profusely illustrated with loads of photos

Plus ... The fans rate the sidekick, and bonus articles on Russell Hayden and Jimmy Ellison—plus much more.

THIS BOOK WOULD MAKE GABBY PROUD!

$20.00 + $4.00 s/h in USA

SMILEY BURNETTE
We Called Him Frog

by Bobby J. Copeland
and Richard B. Smith, III

$18.00 + $3.00 s/h in USA

You will learn all about SMILEY BURNETTE, one of B-Western's premier comics:

- How he got the name Smiley.
- His vast music contribution to his films.
- What Smiley thought of Gene Autry.
- Comments by those who loved him, and those who didn't.
- Film historians' opinions of his place in Western film history.
- His roles in his many films.
- Many great photos.

Plus ... A lot about Gene Autry's strikes against Republic, Pat Buttram's near death experience, etc.

You will never know the whole SUNSET CARSON story until you read this book.
- His life — good and bad.
- The truth about his real name and birth date.
- Sunset talks about himself and his fellow actors.
- Remarks by actors with whom he worked.
- Fans' and writers' opinions of Sunset and his movies.
- Filmography and his films in detail.
- Loaded with photos.

After reading this book you will have a greater appreciation of B-Westerns' tallest star.

SUNSET CARSON
The Adventures of a Cowboy Hero

by Bobby J. Copeland
and Richard B. Smith, III

$18.00 + $3.00 s/h in USA

EMPIRE PUBLISHING, INC. • 3130 US HIGHWAY 220 • MADISON, NC 27025 • PHONE 336-427-5850 • FAX 336-427-7372

The ROUND-UP

A Pictorial History of WESTERN Movie & Television STARS Through the Years!

by Donald Key

"This book brings back memories for me... makes me think back to those days at Republic."
—Monte Hale

Relive those treasured Saturday afternoons of your youth when you cheered on your favorite B-Western cowboy heroes: Tom Mix, Hoot Gibson, Ken Maynard, Tim McCoy, Gene Autry, Dale Evans, Roy Rogers, Lash LaRue, the Durango Kid, Buck Jones, Hopalong Cassidy, Wild Bill Elliott, Sunset Carson. And bring back memories of the Classic TV-Western cowboys and the more recent A-Western stars.

They're all here in what may be the mot comprehensive (and attractive) Western star picture book ever produced. You get 298 heroes, heroines, stuntmen, sidekicks, villains, and cattlepunchers, plus 2 musical groups (the Cass County Boys and the Sons of the Pioneers). From old-time stuntman Art Acord to Tony Young (who played Cord in TV's *Gunslinger)*, from Harry Carey to Clint Eastwood, this handsome volume includes all your favorites from the turn of the century through the 1990s, arranged in alphabetical order for easy reference. But this is more than just a pictorial. Each full-page entry includes a discretely placed one-paragraph background summary of the actor of group, with dates of birth and death. PLUS you get all these EXTRAS:

- Revised 2005
- Foreword by Monte Hale
- Afterword by Neil Summers
- Bibliography
- Quality hardcover to withstand repeated use.

$27.00 + $4.00 s/h

"As time marches on, and so many of our screen and personal friends leave us, books like The Round-Up become even more important to us and to the history of Westerns."
—Neil Summers

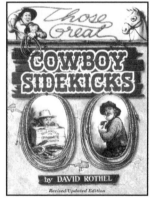

Those Great COWBOY SIDEKICKS
by David Rothel

- 8-1/2 x 11
- Beautiful color cover
- 300+ pages
- Over 200 photos

$25.00 + $4.00 s/h

This book features in-depth profiles of such fondly-remembered character actors as George "Gabby" Hayes, Smiley Burnette, Andy Devine, Al "Fuzzy" St. John, Pat Buttram, Max Terhune, Fuzzy Knight, and many other sidekicks of the B-Westerns—thirty-nine in all! Much of Those Great Cowboy Sidekicks is told through the reminiscences of the sidekicks themselves and the cowboy stars who enjoyed the company of these often bewhiskered, tobacco-chewing saddle pals. Mr. Rothel provides the reader with the rare opportunity to go behind the scenes to discover the manner in which Western screen comedy was created.

Author David Rothel is a Western film historian who has also written AN AMBUSH OF GHOSTS, RIM HOLT, RICHARD BOONE: A KNIGHT WITHOUT ARMOR IN A SAVAGE LAND, THE ROY ROGERS BOOK, THE GENE AUTRY BOOK, and several other titles.

EMPIRE PUBLISHING, INC. • PO BOX 717 • MADISON, NC 27025 • PH 336-427-5850 • FAX 336-427-7372

Other Fine Western Books Available from Empire Publishing, Inc:

ABC's of Movie Cowboys by Edgar M. Wyatt. $5.00.
Art Acord and the Movies by Grange B. McKinney. $15.00.
Audie Murphy: Now Showing by Sue Gossett. $30.00.
Back in the Saddle: Essays on Western Film and Television Actors edited by Garry Yoggy. $29.95.
Best of the Badmen by Boyd Magers, Bobby Copeland, and Bob Nareau. $39.00.
Brothers of the West: The Lives and Films of Robert Livingston and Jack Randall by Merrill McCord. $34.95.
B-Western Actors Encyclopedia by Ted Holland. $30.00.
B-Western Boot Hill: A Final Tribute to the Cowboys and Cowgirls Who Rode the Saturday Matinee Movie Range by Bobby Copeland. $15.00.
Charlie King: We Called Him Blackie by Bobby Copeland. $15.00.
Crusaders of the Sagebrush by Hank Williams. $29.95.
Duke, The Life and Image of John Wayne by Ronald L. Davis. $14.95.
The Films and Career of Audie Murphy by Sue Gossett. $18.00.
The First Fifty Years of Sound Western Movie Locations by Kenny Stier. $34.95.
Gabby Hayes: King of the Cowboy Comics by Bobby J. Copeland and Richard B. Smith, III. $20.00.
The Golden Corral, A Roundup of Magnificent Western Films by Ed Andreychuk. $29.95.
The Hollywood Posse, The Story of a Gallant Band of Horsemen Who Made Movie History by Diana Serra Cary. $16.95.
In a Door, Into a Fight, Out a Door, Into a Chase, Movie-Making Remembered by the Guy at the Door by William Witney. $24.95.
John Ford, Hollywood's Old Master by Ronald L. Davis. $14.95.
John Wayne—Actor, Artist, Hero by Richard D. McGhee. $27.50.
John Wayne, An American Legend by Roger M. Crowley. $29.95.
Johnny Mack Brown—Up Close and Personal by Bobby Copeland. $20.00.
Kid Kowboys: Juveniles in Western Films by Bob Nareau. $20.00.
Ladies of the Western by Boyd Magers and Michael G. Fitzgerald. $35.00.
Lash LaRue, King of the Bullwhip by Chuck Thornton and David Rothel. $25.00.
Last of the Cowboy Heroes by Budd Boetticher. $28.50.
More Cowboy Shooting Stars by John A. Rutherford and Richard B. Smith, III. $18.00.
The Official TV Western Roundup Book by Neil Summers and Roger M. Crowley. $34.95.
Randolph Scott, A Film Biography by Jefferson Brim Crow, III. $25.00.
Richard Boone: A Knight Without Armor in a Savage Land by David Rothel. $30.00.
Riding the (Silver Screen) Range, The Ultimate Western Movie Trivia Book by Ann Snuggs. $15.00.
Riding the Video Range, The Rise and Fall of the Western on Television by Garry A. Yoggy. $75.00.
The Round-Up, A Pictorial History of Western Movie and Television Stars Through the Years by Donald R. Key. $27.00.
Roy Rogers, A Biography, Radio History, Television Career Chronicle, Discography, Filmography, etc. by Robert W. Phillips. $75.00.
Roy Barcroft: King of the Badmen by Bobby Copeland. $15.00.
The Roy Rogers Reference-Trivia-Scrapbook by David Rothel. $25.00.
Saddle Gals, A Filmography of Female Players in B-Westerns of the Sound Era by Edgar M. Wyatt and Steve Turner. $10.00.
Silent Hoofbeats: A Salute to the Horses and Riders of the Bygone B-Western Era by Bobby Copeland. $20.00.
Singing in the Saddle by Douglas B. Green. $34.95.
Sixty Great Cowboy Movie Posters by Bruce Hershenson. $14.99.
Smiley Burnette: We Called Him Frog by Bobby J. Copeland and Richard B. Smith, III. $18.00.
The Sons of the Pioneers by Bill O'Neal and Fred Goodwin. $26.95.
So You Wanna See Cowboy Stuff? by Boyd Magers. $25.00.
Sunset Carson: The Adventures of a Cowboy Hero by Bobby J. Copeland and Richard B. Smith, III. $18.00
Tex Ritter: America's Most Beloved Cowboy by Bill O'Neal. $21.95.
Those Great Cowboy Sidekicks by David Rothel. $25.00.
Trail Talk, Candid Comments and Quotes by Performers and Participants of The Saturday Matinee Western Films by Bobby Copeland. $12.50.
The Western Films of Sunset Carson by Bob Carman and Dan Scapperotti. $20.00.
Western Movies: A TV and Video Guide to 4200 Genre Films compiled by Michael R. Pitts. $35.00.
Westerns Women by Boyd Magers and Michael G. Fitzgerald. $35.00.
Written, Produced, and Directed by Oliver Drake. $30.00.

Add $4.00 shipping/handling for first book + $1.00 for each additional book ordered.
Empire Publishing, Inc. • 3130 US Highway 220 • Madison, NC 27025-8306 • Phone 336-427-5850

Publish Your Book THE EASY WAY!

- Plan, Typeset, Proofread, Layout.

- Will Completely Produce Your Book from Start to Finish.

- Will Get Your Book Copyrighted in Your Name and Cataloged in the Library of Congress.

Affordable Prices • Free Price List

We can make your dream come true.

EMPIRE PUBLISHING, INC. (since 1974)

3130 US Highway 220 • Madison, NC 27025
Phone: 336-427-5850 • Fax: 336-427-7372
Email: info@empirepublishinginc.com